QuickCook

QuickCook
Moroccan

Recipes by Ghillie Basan

Every dish, three ways—you choose!
30 minutes | 20 minutes | 10 minutes

Introduction

30 20 10—Quick, Quicker, Quickest

This book offers a new and flexible approach to planning meals for busy cooks, letting you choose the recipe option that best fits the time you have available. Inside you will find 360 dishes that will inspire and motivate you to get cooking every day of the year. All the recipes take a maximum of 30 minutes to cook. Some take as little as 20 minutes and, amazingly, many take only 10 minutes. With a little preparation, you can easily try out one new recipe from this book each night, and slowly you will be able to build a wide and exciting portfolio of recipes to suit your needs.

How Does it Work?

Every recipe in the QuickCook series can be cooked one of three ways—a 30-minute version, a 20-minute version, or a superquick-and-easy 10-minute version. At the beginning of each chapter, you'll find recipes listed by time. Choose a dish based on how much time you have and turn to that page.

You'll find the main recipe in the middle of the page accompanied by a beautiful photograph, as well as two time-variation recipes below.

If you enjoy your chosen dish, why not go back and cook the other time-variation options at a later date? So, if you liked the 20-minute Roasted Chile and Preserved Lemon Sardines, but only have 10 minutes to spare this time around, you'll find a way to cook it using quick ingredients or clever shortcuts.

If you love the ingredients and flavors of the 10-minute Simple Fresh Fruit Kebabs, why not try something more substantial, such as the 20-minute Chilled Rose Water Fruit Salad, or be inspired to make a more elaborate version, such as the Poached Red Wine and Rose Water Fruit? Alternatively, browse through all 360 delicious recipes, find something that catches your eye—then cook the version that fits your time frame.

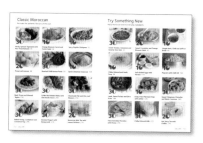

Or, for easy inspiration, turn to the recipe gallery on pages 12–19 to get an instant overview by themes, such as Classic Moroccan or Try Something New.

QuickCook Online

To make life easier, you can use the special code on each recipe page to e-mail yourself a recipe card for printing, or e-mail a text-only shopping list to your phone. Go to www.hamlynquickcook.com and enter the recipe code at the bottom of each page.

MOR-GRIL-GIM

QuickCook Moroccan

Moroccan food is truly a feast for the senses—fragrant, fiery, sweet, and salty. Fruity, syrupy tagines, buttery couscous with scented broths, crispy pastries, tangy salads, and spicy sauces, this is a cuisine that reflects a colorful history of different peoples and their culinary cultures.

Geographically, perched at the northwest corner of the African continent, Morocco acts as a culinary gateway to the native influences of central and northern Africa, to the ancient and medieval traditions of the Arab world to the east, and to the Andalusian flavors of southern Spain across the water. When the Arabs took over the region between the 7th and 14th centuries, they brought spices, nuts, and dried fruits, and they also brought Islam and its dietary restrictions. When the Moors were expelled from Spain, they returned with olives, olive oil, tomatoes, and paprika, while the the Jewish refugees fleeing the Spanish Inquisition brought their valuable preserving techniques, such as the ubiquitous preserved lemons. The French, who colonized parts of Morocco, also left their stamp on the cooking as well as winemaking and their language.

Rich in culture and produce, Morocco weaves the medieval with the modern, from the mountaintop villages to the majestic cities of ancient dynasties and from the deserts with their date-palm oases to the coastline fringed with sun-drenched tourist beaches. This is true of the culinary culture, too—medieval recipes with modern twists, a unique blend of the sensual and the exotic.

Traditions of Moroccan Food

The influence of Islam on Morocco's population does have an effect on the method of killing and preparation of meat (Muslims don't eat pork) and the consumption of alcoholic beverages. However, Morocco is home to a variety of religions and tribal people and does produce its own wines and aperitifs. Morocco is famous for its steaming glasses of sweet mint tea, which is offered as a traditional mark of hospitality. The tea itself is simple to make, but the ceremony surrounding it is important. It is presented in an elaborate teapot, which is held high to pour the steaming amber liquid into glasses so that a little foam forms on the surface, and milk is never added.

Coffee, on the other hand, is more of a café beverage, or reserved for special occasions, and it is served black, spiked with aromatic cardamom seeds or cinnamon sticks, in small cups.

The souks and the old medinas are the lungs of Morocco's culinary culture. Magical and enticing, filled with arresting aromas and colorful displays, they are bustling venues for haggling, meal planning, and snacking. Everything you need to make a meal is available in the street markets: dried apricots, dates, prunes and figs; roasted almonds, walnuts, and pistachios; big bunches of flat leaf parsley, mint and fresh cilantro; containers of spices and dried herbs; vats of olives, bottles of oils, and jars of pickles and preserves; the distilled waters of rose petals and orange blossom; sacks of flour, grains, and couscous; earthenware tagines with their conical lids; and large copper k'dras for celebratory feasts.

A predominant feature of Moroccan cooking, a tagine is essentially a glorified slow-cooked stew, deeply aromatic and full of flavor. The word "tagine" is both the name of the cooked dish and of the cooking vessel. Placed over a charcoal stove, which disperses the heat all around the bottom, a tagine enables the ingredients to cook gently in the steam, which builds up inside the lid, so that they remain tender and moist. A tagine is usually served from the cooking vessel with bread to mop up all the delectable juices, or with couscous.

The word "couscous" refers to the granules as well as the cooked dish, which is traditionally prepared in a "couscoussier"— a two-tiered pot with a stewing section at the bottom for the meat, beans, or vegetables, and a steaming pot on top for the couscous. Couscous is Morocco's national dish, and the preparation of it is such an important part of the culinary life that it determines the status of a cook's ability. Although referred to as a "grain," technically, it is not one; instead, it could be described as Moroccan "pasta," because it is made with semolina flour mixed with water and hand-rolled to different sizes.

For the recipes in *QuickCook Moroccan*, the store-bought couscous granules have already been steamed and dried so they can be prepared quickly; the tagines have been adapted to suit quicker cooking times; and some traditional pickle and preserve recipes have been included because they play a key role in Moroccan cuisine—it is important to note that the method is quick but time for preserving is required, although many are available prepared for Middle Eastern stores and online sources.

A Moroccan Meal

Family and food play a big role in Moroccan life and there are many religious and celebratory occasions for festive feasts. Most Moroccan meals begin with a selection of little dishes, ranging from a simple bowl of marinated olives to pureed vegetable dips, savory pastries, and tangy fruit and vegetable salads, which are served to whet the appetite. A bowl of soup or a tagine might follow, served with a mound of couscous or freshly baked bread. Alternatively, the couscous may be served as a course on its own. Grilled or roasted meat, chicken, or fish might follow and fresh fruit usually completes the meal. On special occasions, the meal will end with a dessert, but most sweet dishes are enjoyed on their own at different times of the day, or they are served as offerings of hospitality and reserved for celebratory feasts. Once the meal is over, glasses of steaming mint tea will be served to aid digestion.

QuickCook Ingredients

Argan oil: Dark in color with a reddish tinge and nutty flavor, this is the main cooking oil of the southern region of Morocco, where the stout, thorny argan trees grow. The goats climb the trees and eat the fleshy exterior of the fruit, which resemble large green olives, and then excrete the nut. The herders or village women collect the nuts and crack them open to extract the kernels, which are then roasted and ground to extract the oil.
Bread: In general, bread is made daily in traditional community ovens and, in rural communities, it is served with every meal to act as a scoop and as a mop to soak up all the delectable sauces. There are a variety of Moroccan breads but the most common are flatbreads, semolina rolls, and baguette-style loaves.
Chermoula: Prepared predominantly with chiles, garlic, cumin seeds, lemon juice, and fresh cilantro, chermoula is used as a marinade or sauce for grilled fish and poultry dishes, and some tagines. Quantities and ingredients vary from region to region.

Dukkah: Originally from Egypt, this coarsely ground nut, seed, and spice mix is often combined with oil to form a dip for bread or vegetables. The basic mix consists of roasted hazelnuts, sesame seeds, and roasted cumin and coriander seeds. Dried chiles, paprika, dried mint, and dried thyme are often added, too.

Harissa: Prepared by pounding dried red chiles that have been soaked in water, or chiles roasted in oil, with spices and fresh cilantro, harissa is a fiery paste. It is served as a condiment to accompany meat, fish, and vegetable dishes; it is added to marinades and sauces; and it is blended with yogurt or olive oil to make a delicious dip.

Preserved lemons: The small, native, thin-skin lemons are preserved in salt and lemon juice, and only the finely chopped or sliced rind is used for cooking and garnishing to impart a distinctive citrus flavor to tagines, grilled dishes, and salads.

Ras el hanout: Translated from Arabic as "head of the shop," this is a delightful medley of 30–40 different spices, some of which are indigenous to the region. Beyond the souks of Morocco, it is difficult to make an authentic ras el hanout, but you can create your own versions by grinding together equal quantities of peppercorns, cloves, nigella seeds, allspice berries, mace, coriander seeds, and cumin seeds, and then adding ground ginger, ground cinnamon, dried lavender, and dried rose petals.

Smen: An acquired taste, smen is an aged butter with a rancid flavor. Set in earthenware pots and stored in a cool, dry place for months, it is regarded as an essential component in some tagines. A good substitute is ghee, which is clarified butter and, although it has a warm aroma and a nutty flavor instead of the pungent one of smen, it gives the same kind of depth to a dish. To make your own clarified butter, heat butter over medium-low heat until the milk solids separate and skim off the milky residue.

Tabil: This is a North African spice mix that is often used to flavor grilled dishes and street food. To make your own, grind equal quantities of coriander seeds, caraway seeds, dried chile, and salt, to which you can add roasted crushed garlic and roasted chickpeas, and sesame seeds.

Zahtar: Originally from the Middle East, this is a popular street spice used for sprinkling over grilled and fried food and savory pastries. To make your own, combine equal quantities of roasted sesame seeds and dried thyme with sumac and a little sea salt.

Classic Moroccan

Recreate the authentic flavors of the souk.

Herbed Spinach Tapenade with Pan-Fried Cheese 30

Orange Blossom Carrot and Cumin Salad 34

Spicy Paprika Chickpeas 52

Preserved Lemons 68

Roasted Chile Harissa Paste 70

Quick Cinnamon Couscous 128

Beef, Prune, and Almond Tagine 150

Broiled Red Snapper Fillets with Chermoula Sauce 200

Chermoula Fish and Grape Leaf Skewers 214

Baked Honey, Cardamom, and Cinnamon Figs 246

Strained Yogurt with Honeycomb 270

Moroccan Mint Tea with Lemon Verbena 274

Try Something New

Add a Moroccan twist to everyday ingredients.

Sweet Tomato, Cinnamon, and Sesame Seed Jam 32

Sweet Cucumber and Orange Blossom Salad 42

Simple Herb, Chile, and Saffron Broth 90

Chilled Almond and Garlic Soup 94

Soft-Boiled Eggs with Harissa 114

Popcorn with Chili Oil 120

Lamb, Sweet Potato, and Okra K'dra 148

Deep-Fried Plantain Chips with Zahtar 226

Sweet Cinnamon, Pistachio, and Raisin Couscous 240

Semolina Pancakes with Honey 256

Chilled Almond Milk 272

Hot Spicy Tea with Chiles 276

Chicken and Poultry

Satisfying dinners steeped with warm and aromatic flavors.

**Honeyed Pumpkin and
Ginger Broth** 78

**Minty Chicken and
Rice Soup** 88

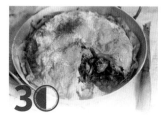

**Chicken, Nut, and
Cinnamon Pie** 100

**Chicken, Green Olive, and
Preserved Lemon Tagine** 144

**Cinnamon Duck and
Caramelized Pear Tagine** 158

**Herbed Carrot, Potato,
and Pea Tagine** 164

**Saffron, Onion, Chicken,
Turnip, and Chickpea K'dra** 174

**Roasted Cinnamon Chicken
Thighs and Plums** 190

**Roasted Honeyed Quince
and Duck Legs** 192

**Pan-Fried Quails with
Ginger and Grapes** 194

**Chargrilled Harissa Chicken
Wings with Burned Oranges** 196

**Chicken Livers and Pomegranate
Syrup on Fried Bread** 198

Meaty Treats

Hearty dishes to warm your soul.

Lamb, Chickpea, and
Cinnamon Broth 80

Lemony Beef, Bean,
and Cumin Soup 82

Mini Lamb and
Harissa Pizzas 106

Chorizo and Parsley Eggs 108

Couscous Tfaia with Beef 132

Cardamom Lamb
and Dates 160

Chorizo, Lentil, and
Fenugreek Tagine 162

Moroccan Onion
and Lamb Kebabs 180

Moroccan Onion and
Cumin Beef Burgers 182

Fennel-Roasted Lamb
with Honeyed Figs 184

Spicy Chargrilled Meatballs
with Toasted Coconut 186

Spicy Pan-Fried Liver,
Prunes, and Onions 188

Veggie Delights

A feast of flavors to add color to your table.

Onion, Parsley, Tomato, and
Pomegranate Syrup Salad 36

Herbed Tomato, Caper, and
Preserved Lemon Salad 40

Warm Garlicky Lentil Salad 50

Tomato, Ras el Hanout,
and Vermicelli Soup 76

Carrot, Cilantro, and
Lentil Soup 92

Zucchini, Mint, and
Bread Omelet 110

Chile and Herb Sweet
Potato Pancakes 112

Couscous with Spring
Vegetables and Dill 134

Three Bell Pepper, Olive, Feta,
and Egg Tagine 166

Ras el Hanout Lentils
and Chickpeas 172

Vegetable Kebabs with
Harissa Yogurt 216

Roasted Spiced Squash 224

Fish and Seafood

Spicy seafood to turn up the heat.

Fino, Harissa, and Roasted Pepper Fish Soup 84

Mussel, Chile, and Cilantro Broth 86

Deep-Fried Fish and Chermoula Pastries 104

Lemon Couscous with Spicy Shellfish 138

Chermoula Monkfish and Black Olive Tagine 146

Toasted Saffron, Herb, and Preserved Lemon Fish Tagine 154

Herbed Shrimp, Tomato, and Turmeric Fennel Tagine 156

Seared Harissa Tuna Steaks 204

Swordfish, Bay, and Lime Kebabs 206

Grilled Turmeric Squid with Crushed Chickpeas 208

Chargrilled Chile Shrimp with Lime 210

Mini Saffron Fish Balls 212

Fruity Dishes

Tempting dishes bursting with fragrance.

Olive, Caper, and Bitter Orange Relish 24

Pink Grapefruit and Fennel Salad 38

Artichoke, Clementine, and Preserved Lemon Salad 46

Beet, Apple, and Orange Blossom Salad 48

Apple and Butternut Soup with Chili Oil 96

Chile, Lime, and Cilantro Dried Fruit and Nuts 116

Spicy Pine Nut and Apricot Couscous 130

Ginger and Honey Lamb and Apricot Tagine 140

Spicy Zucchini, Eggplant, and Date Tagine 168

Watermelon, Rose Water, and Lemon Balm Salad 232

Hot Spiced Dried Fruit Compote 250

Simple Fresh Fruit Kebabs 252

Great for Entertaining

Indulgent dishes designed to impress.

2 Pear, Endive, and
Rose Petal Salad 60

3 Chile and Fino Gazpacho 98

3 Parsnip and Beet Chips with
Homemade Dukkah 118

3 Cheese and Paprika
Potato Cakes 122

3 Couscous with Orangey
Fennel and Zucchini 136

1 Spicy Beef, Sun-Dried
Tomatoes, and Pine Nuts 142

2 Roasted Chile and Preserved
Lemon Sardines 202

3 Roasted Cilantro and Preserved
Lemon Potatoes 222

2 Date and Pistachio Truffles 238

1 Crystallized Rose Petals 258

3 Saffron Pears with Honey
and Lavender 264

1 Moroccan Coffee with
Cardamom 278

QuickCook

Appetizers, Salads, Pickles, and Preserves

Recipes listed by cooking time

30

20

10

20 Olive, Caper, and Bitter Orange Relish

Serves 4

2 tomatoes

1½ cups fleshy black ripe olives, pitted and coarsely chopped

finely chopped rind of 1 small fresh or preserved bitter orange

2 garlic cloves, crushed

1 scant teaspoon ground cumin

1 tablespoon baby capers, rinsed and drained

1 tablespoon olive oil

salt and black pepper

toasted flatbreads, to serve (optional)

- Put the tomatoes in a heatproof bowl and pour enough boiling water over them to cover. Let stand for 1–2 minutes, then drain, cut a cross at the stem end of each tomato, and peel off the skins. Cut into quarters, remove the seeds, and coarsely chop the flesh.

- Put the chopped tomatoes and olives into a bowl. Add the orange rind, garlic, and cumin and season. Stir in the capers, then add the oil and mix well. Let stand for at least 10 minutes before serving, with toasted flatbreads, if desired.

 **Orangy Spiced Olives**

Put 3½ cups rinsed and drained cracked green olives into a bowl. Dry-fry 1 teaspoon each of cumin seeds, coriander seeds, and cardamom seeds and ½ teaspoon black peppercorns in a small, heavy skillet over medium heat for 1–2 minutes, until they emit a nutty aroma. Using a mortar and pestle, crush the spices, then add to the olives with 2–3 tablespoons olive oil, the juice of 1 orange, and 1–2 teaspoons harissa paste (see page 70). Mix well and serve. (The olives can also be stored in a sealed sterilized jar in the refrigerator for up to 2 weeks.)

 Olive, Feta, and Bitter Orange Salad Using a sharp knife, pit 4½ cups fleshy green olives and cut into slivers, then transfer to a bowl. Dry-fry 2 teaspoons coriander seeds in a small, heavy skillet over medium heat for 2 minutes, until they emit a nutty aroma. Using a mortar and pestle, crush the seeds, then add to the olives with the finely sliced rind of 1 fresh or preserved bitter orange. Toss with 2 tablespoons olive oil and 1 tablespoon balsamic vinegar, then let stand for at least 10 minutes to let the flavors mingle. Sprinkle with ⅔ cup crumbled feta cheese and serve with chunks of warm crusty bread.

10 Harissa Eggplant with Goat Cheese Toasts

Serves 4

2–3 tablespoons olive or argan oil

1 eggplant, diced

2 teaspoons harissa paste
(see page 70)

1–2 tablespoons water

1 teaspoon sugar

1 tablespoon finely chopped
flat leaf parsley

salt and black pepper

To serve

creamy or crumbly goat cheese

toasted flatbreads

• Heat the oil in a heavy skillet, stir in the eggplant, and cook for 2–3 minutes, until lightly browned. Stir in the harissa and mix well.

• Add the measured water and sugar and cook for another 2–3 minutes. Season and sprinkle with the parsley. Serve with creamy or crumbly goat cheese on toasted flatbreads.

---

2 Chargrilled Eggplant and Harissa Dip

Using tongs, hold 2 eggplants over a gas flame and cook for 10–12 minutes, turning occasionally, until the skin begins to char and flake—it may even burst in places. When soft, place in a plastic food bag to sweat for 2–3 minutes. Hold by the stems under cold running water and gently peel off the skin. Squeeze out any excess water and place on a board. Remove the stems, then chop the flesh to a pulp and transfer to a bowl. Add 3–4 tablespoons thick, plain yogurt, 2 teaspoons harissa paste (see page 70), and 1–2 tablespoons finely chopped cilantro. Season and mix well. Serve with bread.

3 Eggplant, Harissa, and Tomato Dip

Put 2 peeled and cubed eggplants into a steamer and steam for 8–10 minutes, until soft. Transfer to a board and mash with a fork. Heat 2–3 tablespoons olive oil in a heavy saucepan, stir in 1–2 teaspoons cumin seeds and 2–3 crushed garlic cloves, and cook until fragrant. Add 1 (14½ oz) can diced tomatoes, drained of juice, 1–2 teaspoons each of sugar and harissa paste (see page 70), and 2 tablespoons finely chopped flat leaf parsley and cook over low heat for 10–15 minutes, until thickened. Stir in the juice of 1 lemon and the mashed eggplants, mix well, and heat through. Season to taste. Garnish with a little more finely chopped parsley and serve warm or at room temperature with chunks of crusty bread.

2 Fava Bean Dip with Preserved Lemon

Serves 4

4½–6 cups shelled fresh
  fava beans
2–3 garlic cloves, halved
1–2 teaspoons ground cumin
1 teaspoon ground coriander
3 tablespoons olive oil
juice of ½ lemon
1–2 teaspoons finely chopped
  preserved lemon rind
  (see page 68)
salt and black pepper
toasted flatbreads or vegetable
  sticks, to serve

- Cook the fava beans in a saucepan of boiling water for 3–4 minutes, until tender. Drain, then slip the larger beans out of their tough skins (the smaller beans don't need to be skinned).

- Using a large mortar and pestle, pound the beans, garlic, and ground spices to a smooth paste. Alternatively, process in a food processor. Gradually mix in the oil and lemon juice to form a smooth puree, then season well.

- Transfer the puree to a serving bowl and sprinkle with the preserved lemon rind. Serve warm or at room temperature with toasted flatbreads or vegetables sticks.

---

1 Fava Bean, Preserved Lemon, and Mint Salad Cook 4½ cups shelled fresh or frozen fava beans in a saucepan of boiling water for 3–4 minutes, until tender. Drain and refresh under cold running water, then slip the beans out of their tough skins. Transfer the beans to a bowl and toss with 2 tablespoons olive oil and 1 tablespoon balsamic vinegar. Add 1–2 teaspoons finely sliced preserved lemon rind (see page 68) and a finely shredded small bunch of mint leaves. Season well and serve.

3 Fava Bean, Carrot, Preserved Lemon, and Egg Salad Cook 3 cups shelled fresh or frozen fava beans in a saucepan of boiling water for 3–4 minutes, until tender. Drain and refresh under cold running water, then slip the larger beans out of their skins and set all the beans aside. Steam 2–3 peeled and sliced carrots for 5 minutes or until tender but not soft. Drain and refresh under cold running water. Put the beans, carrots, and 1 red onion, cut into bite-size pieces, into a bowl and add the finely sliced rind of 1 preserved lemon (see page 68) and a coarsely chopped small bunch of flat leaf parsley. Mix together 2 tablespoons olive or argan oil, the juice of 1 lemon, 2 crushed garlic cloves, and 1 teaspoon crushed cumin seeds and season. Pour over the salad and toss well, then spoon onto a serving dish. Cook 3–4 eggs in a saucepan of boiling water for about 4 minutes, then drain and shell. Cut into quarters and arrange on the salad. Sprinkle with a little paprika and serve while the eggs are still warm.

30 Herbed Spinach Tapenade with Pan-Fried Cheese

Serves 4

1 (6 oz) package baby spinach
    leaves
handful of celery leaves
2 tablespoons olive oil
2–3 garlic cloves, crushed
1 teaspoon cumin seeds
6–8 black ripe olives,
    pitted and finely chopped
large bunch of flat leaf parsley,
    finely chopped
large bunch of cilantro,
    finely chopped
1 teaspoon Spanish smoked paprika
juice of ½ lemon
salt and black pepper

For the fried cheese

2 tablespoons olive oil
8 oz Muenster or haloumi
    cheese, sliced

- Place the spinach and celery leaves in a steamer and cook for 10–15 minutes, until soft. Refresh under cold running water, then drain well and squeeze out the excess water. Chop to a fine pulp.

- Heat the oil in a heavy skillet, stir in the garlic and cumin seeds, and cook until they emit a nutty aroma. Stir in the olives, parsley, cilantro, and paprika. Add the spinach and celery leaves, season well, and cook gently for 8–10 minutes, until the mixture is smooth.

- Meanwhile, cook the cheese. Heat the oil in a separate heavy skillet, add the Muenster cheese, and cook for 3–4 minutes, turning once, until golden brown and crispy. Drain on paper towels.

- Transfer the spinach mixture to a bowl, add the lemon juice, and mix well. Serve warm with the fried cheese and garnished with lemon wedges, if desired.

 ### Spinach and Herb Yogurt

Steam 1 (6 oz) package baby spinach leaves with a small bunch each of flat leaf parsley and mint leaves for about 8 minutes, or until soft. Meanwhile, beat together 1 cup thick, plain yogurt, 2 crushed garlic cloves, and 1 scant teaspoon ground cumin in a bowl and season well. Squeeze out the excess water from the cooked spinach and herbs, then beat into the yogurt. Serve with chunks of warm crusty bread.

 ### Sautéed Spinach and Herbs

Rinse and drain 1 (5 oz) package spinach leaves, a large bunch of arugula leaves, and a large bunch each of flat leaf parsley, mint, and cilantro, then coarsely chop together. Heat 2–3 tablespoons olive oil in a large, heavy skillet, stir in 2 crushed garlic cloves and 1–2 finely chopped green chiles, and cook for 1–2 minutes, until beginning to brown. Toss in the spinach mixture and cook gently until just wilted. Add the finely chopped rind of ½ preserved lemon (see page 68) and season to taste. Serve warm on toasted bread with dollops of thick, plain yogurt.

3 Sweet Tomato, Cinnamon, and Sesame Seed Jam

Serves 4

6–8 large ripe tomatoes
2–3 tablespoons olive oil
1 tablespoon tomato paste
2 tablespoons honey
1 teaspoon ground cinnamon
1 teaspoon ground ginger
1 tablespoon sesame seeds
salt and black pepper
crusty bread, to serve

- Place the tomatoes in an ovenproof dish, pour the oil over them, and roast in a preheated oven, at 400°F, for 15 minutes. Remove the tomatoes with a slotted spoon, reserving the oil. Peel off the skins and chop to a pulp.

- Transfer the tomatoes to a heavy saucepan with the tomato paste and 1 tablespoon of the roasting oil and cook over high heat until bubbling. Stir in the honey, cinnamon, and ginger and cook for another 5–10 minutes, until the mixture is thick, adding more of the oil, if necessary.

- Meanwhile, dry-fry the sesame seeds in a small, heavy skillet over medium heat for 2–3 minutes, until golden brown.

- Season the preserves, transfer to a serving bowl, and sprinkle with the toasted sesame seeds. Serve warm or at room temperature with crusty bread for dipping.

 Spicy Tomato and Sesame Seed Paste Drain and pat dry 1 cup sun-dried tomatoes in oil. Using a large mortar and pestle, pound the tomatoes, 2–3 garlic cloves, and 1 teaspoon each of ground cumin, ground cinnamon, ground cardamom, and harissa paste (see page 70) to a paste. Season with salt and mix with a little olive oil. Alternatively, process in a food processor. Spoon into a bowl, sprinkle with 1–2 teaspoons toasted sesame seeds, and serve with chunks of crusty bread.

 Dried Tomato, Feta, and Sesame Seed Salad Drain and pat dry 1 cup sun-dried tomatoes in oil, then finely slice and put into a bowl. Add 7 oz feta cheese, cubed, and the finely sliced rind of 1 preserved lemon (see page 68). In a separate bowl, mix together 2–3 tablespoons olive or argan oil, the juice of 1 lemon, and 1 teaspoon each of crushed coriander seeds, crushed fennel seeds, and finely chopped dried red chile, then pour the dressing over the salad and let stand for 5–10 minutes. Serve sprinkled with 2 teaspoons toasted sesame seeds.

Orange Blossom Carrot and Cumin Salad

Serves 4

juice of 1 lemon
2 tablespoons orange
   blossom water
½ teaspoon ground cumin
1 teaspoon honey or sugar
8 carrots, peeled and shredded
salt
ground cinnamon, for dusting

- Mix together the lemon juice, orange blossom water, cumin, and honey or sugar in a bowl.

- Put the shredded carrots in a serving bowl and pour over the dressing. Season with salt and toss well. Sprinkle with a little cinnamon before serving.

 Warm Carrot and Toasted Cumin Salad Put 8 carrots, peeled and cut into sticks, into a steamer and steam for 10–12 minutes, until tender but not mushy. Meanwhile, dry-fry 1–2 teaspoons cumin seeds in a small, heavy skillet over medium heat for 2 minutes, until they emit a nutty aroma. Set aside. Transfer the carrots to a bowl and, while still warm, toss with 2 tablespoons olive or argan oil, the juice of 1 lemon, 2 crushed garlic cloves, the toasted cumin seeds, and 1 teaspoon honey. Season well and let stand for at least 5 minutes to let the flavors mingle. Just before serving, toss in a finely chopped small bunch each of cilantro and mint.

 Herbed Roasted Carrot and Cumin Dip Put 8 carrots, peeled and thickly sliced, in an ovenproof dish and pour ½ cup olive oil over them. Put into a preheated oven, at 400°F, for about 15 minutes. Toss with 2 crushed garlic cloves and 2 teaspoons cumin seeds, then return to the oven and cook for another 10 minutes, until the carrots are tender but not soft. Transfer to a bowl and crush to a coarse paste, using a potato masher. Alternatively, put into a food processor and process to a smooth paste. Mix in the juice of 1 lemon and a finely chopped small bunch each of flat leaf parsley, dill, and mint. Season and spoon into a serving bowl. Drizzle with a little olive oil and garnish with extra chopped herbs. Serve warm or at room temperature with strips of toasted flatbread.

 # Onion, Parsley, Tomato, and Pomegranate Syrup Salad

Serves 4

2 tomatoes
large bunch of flat leaf parsley,
    coarsely chopped
2 red onions, finely sliced
2 teaspoons coriander seeds
finely sliced rind of 1 preserved
    lemon (see page 68)
2 tablespoons pomegranate syrup
salt and black pepper

- Put the tomatoes into a heatproof bowl and pour enough boiling water over them to cover. Let stand for 1–2 minutes, then drain, cut a cross at the stem end of each tomato, and peel off the skins. Cut into quarters, remove the seeds, and coarsely chop the flesh. Place in a serving bowl and add the parsley and onions.

- Dry-fry the coriander seeds in a small, heavy skillet over medium heat for 2 minutes, until they emit a nutty aroma. Using a mortar and pestle, lightly crush the seeds. Add to the tomato mixture with the preserved lemon rind. Pour the pomegranate syrup over the salad and season well. Gently toss together and serve.

---

10 Onion, Parsley, and Pomegranate Syrup Salad Spread 2 finely sliced white onions on a plate and sprinkle with salt. Let stand for 5–8 minutes, then rinse, drain, and pat dry. Put into a serving bowl and stir in a chopped small bunch each of flat leaf parsley and mint and 1–2 teaspoons sumac. Drizzle with 1 tablespoon pomegranate syrup and serve.

30 Parsley, Onion, Walnut, Tomato, and Pomegranate Syrup Salad Evenly chop a large bunch of flat leaf parsley, leaves and stems. Chop 2–3 tablespoons walnuts into bite-size pieces and put, together with the parsley, in a shallow serving bowl. Add 2–3 tomatoes, skinned and seeded as above and chopped to the same size as the walnuts, and 1–2 seeded and finely chopped green chiles, then sprinkle with 1 finely chopped red onion. Drizzle with 2 tablespoons pomegranate syrup and season well with salt. Let stand for 15–20 minutes to let the onion juices seep into the salad. Gently toss together and serve with toasted flatbreads.

3⬤ Pink Grapefruit and Fennel Salad

Serves 4

1 fennel bulb

1 tablespoon olive oil

juice of ½ lemon

1 scant teaspoon cumin seeds,
    crushed

2 pink grapefruit

1 scant teaspoon salt

2–3 scallions, finely sliced

1 tablespoon black ripe olives,
    pitted

- Cut the bottom off the fennel and remove the outer layers. Cut in half lengthwise and in half horizontally, then finely slice with the grain. Place in a bowl and toss with the oil, lemon juice, and cumin seeds. Let marinate for 20 minutes.

- Meanwhile, using a sharp knife, remove the peel and pith from the grapefruit. Holding the grapefruit over a bowl to catch the juice, cut down between the membranes and remove the segments. Cut each segment in half, place in the bowl, and sprinkle with the salt. Let stand for 5 minutes to draw out the sweet juices.

- Add the fennel to the grapefruit and mix in the scallions. Serve topped with the olives.

 Grapefruit and Toasted Fennel Seed Salad Dry-fry 1–2 teaspoons fennel seeds in a small, heavy skillet over medium heat for 2 minutes, until they emit a nutty aroma, then set aside. Using a sharp knife, remove the peel and pith from 2 sweet grapefruits, then cut down between the membranes and remove the segments. Arrange the segments on a plate and sprinkle with 1 tablespoon orange blossom water. Sprinkle the toasted fennel seeds over the salad and serve.

2⬤ **Orange, Fennel, and Apple Salad** Prepare 2 fennel bulbs as above. Put into a bowl and toss with the juice of 1 lemon. Add 2 cored and finely sliced crispy red or green apples and toss to coat well in the lemon juice. Using a sharp knife, remove the peel and pith from 1 orange. Holding the orange over the salad bowl to catch the juice, cut down between the membranes and remove the segments, then add to the bowl. Dry-fry 1–2 tablespoons shelled pistachio nuts in a small, heavy skillet over medium heat for 1–2 minutes, until they begin to brown and emit a nutty aroma. Using a mortar and pestle, pound the pistachios, 1 garlic clove, and a small handful of mint leaves to a coarse paste. Mix with 1–2 tablespoons olive oil, then drizzle the dressing over the salad. Season and toss well.

Herbed Tomato, Caper, and Preserved Lemon Salad

Serves 4

4 large tomatoes

finely sliced rind of 1 preserved
lemon (see page 68)

1 red onion, sliced into
bite-size pieces

1–2 tablespoons baby capers,
rinsed and drained

small bunch of flat leaf parsley,
finely chopped

small bunch of cilantro,
finely chopped

small bunch of mint,
finely chopped

2 tablespoons olive or argan oil

juice of ½ lemon

1 scant teaspoon paprika

salt and black pepper

warm crusty bread, to serve
(optional)

- Put the tomatoes in a heatproof bowl and pour enough boiling water over them to cover. Let stand for 1–2 minutes, then drain, cut a cross at the stem end of each tomato, and peel off the skins. Cut into quarters, remove the seeds, and cut the flesh into thick strips. Put into a large, shallow bowl and add the preserved lemon rind.

- Add the onion, capers, and herbs to the bowl. Gently toss with the oil and lemon juice and season. Sprinkle with the paprika and serve with warm crusty bread, if desired.

Spicy Tomato and Preserved Lemon Salad Thinly slice 4–6 ripe tomatoes and put into a shallow bowl. Add 2 seeded and finely sliced, large green chiles and the finely sliced rind of ½ preserved lemon (see page 68). Drizzle with a little olive or argan oil and season with salt. Gently stir in a finely chopped small bunch of cilantro and serve.

Spicy Roasted Tomatoes with Preserved Lemon Put 3 cups cherry tomatoes into an ovenproof dish and pour 2–3 tablespoons olive oil over them. Place in a preheated oven, at 350°F, for 15 minutes. Add 1–2 finely chopped fresh red chiles or 1–2 teaspoons chopped dried red chile and 1 teaspoon sugar and mix together with the tomatoes and oil. Return to the oven and cook for another 10 minutes, until the tomatoes begin to buckle. Season with salt and spoon into a serving dish. Sprinkle with the finely chopped rind of ½ preserved lemon (see page 68) and garnish with a finely chopped small bunch of cilantro.

MOR-STAR-TOQ

Sweet Cucumber and Orange Blossom Salad

Serves 4

2 cucumbers, peeled and grated
juice of ½ lemon
1–2 tablespoons orange
  blossom water
1–2 teaspoons sugar or honey
salt
½ teaspoon ground cinnamon,
  for dusting

- Put the grated cucumber into a colander, sprinkle with salt, and let stand for about 5 minutes. Using your hands, squeeze out the excess water and put the cucumber into a bowl.

- Mix together the lemon juice, orange blossom water, and sugar or honey in a separate bowl, then pour the dressing over the cucumber. Toss well, cover, and chill for 10 minutes. Just before serving, dust with the cinnamon.

 Salted Cucumber Batons

Peel the skin off 2 cucumbers in strips, leaving some narrow strips on the flesh for decorative effect. Cut into equal thick batons. Place on a plate, sprinkle with 1–2 teaspoons coarse salt, and let stand for 5–6 minutes, until the salt has almost dissolved. Lift the cucumber off the plate, leaving behind any excess liquid, but don't rinse. Arrange in a fan on a serving dish and serve immediately.

 Cucumber, Pomegranate, and Orange Blossom Salad Peel 1 cucumber, cut it into quarters lengthwise, and finely slice. Put into a colander, sprinkle with salt, and let stand for 10 minutes. Meanwhile, cut 1 white onion into bite-size pieces, put into a separate colander, sprinkle with salt, and let stand for 5 minutes. Cut 2 pomegranates into quarters, then, holding them over a plate to catch the juice, bend each quarter backward and flick the seeds into a serving bowl, leaving behind the white membrane and pith (this takes about 10 minutes). Add any pomegranate juice to the bowl. Rinse and drain the cucumber, then squeeze out the excess water. Rinse and drain the onion, then pat dry with paper towels. Add the cucumber and onion to the pomegranate seeds and juice, then toss with 2 tablespoons orange blossom water. Let stand for 5–10 minutes to let the juices mingle with the syrup. Just before serving, toss in 1 tablespoon finely shredded mint.

30 Orange, Date, and Chile Salad

Serves 4

3–4 ripe sweet oranges
6 soft pitted dates, finely sliced
2–3 tablespoons orange
blossom water
1 red chile, seeded and
finely sliced
finely sliced rind of ½ preserved
lemon (see page 68)

- Using a sharp knife, remove the peel and pith from the oranges. Place the oranges on a plate to catch the juice and thinly slice into circles or semicircles, removing any seeds. Place the oranges and juice in a shallow bowl.

- Sprinkle with the dates, then pour the orange blossom water over the fruit. Cover and let stand for 15 minutes to let the flavors mingle and the dates soften.

- Sprinkle with the chile and preserved lemon rind and gently toss together.

 Orange, Olive, and Chile Salad

Using a sharp knife, remove the peel and pith from 3 oranges, then thinly slice into circles or semicircles, removing any seeds, and arrange on a serving plate. Finely slice 1 red onion into circles or semicircles and arrange over the oranges. Drizzle with a little olive oil and season with salt. Sprinkle with 2 tablespoons black ripe olives and garnish with 1 seeded and finely sliced green chile and a finely shredded small bunch of mint.

 Orange, Radish, and Chile Salad

Using a sharp knife, remove the peel and pith from 2–3 oranges. Holding the oranges over a bowl to catch the juice, cut down between the membranes and remove the segments. Cut each segment in half, remove any seeds, and put into the bowl. Dry-fry 2 teaspoons fennel seeds in a small, heavy skillet over medium heat for 2–3 minutes, until they emit a nutty aroma, then sprinkle the seeds over the oranges. Add

6–8 sliced small red radishes, 1 tablespoon pitted and sliced green olives, and 2 seeded and sliced green chiles. Mix together 2 tablespoons olive oil, 1 tablespoon orange blossom water, and 1 teaspoon honey and pour the dressing over the salad. Season, toss together lightly, and serve sprinkled with 1 tablespoon finely chopped parsley.

 # Artichoke, Clementine, and Preserved Lemon Salad

Serves 4

4 canned artichoke hearts, rinsed and drained

3–4 sweet clementines, peeled and pith removed

1–2 tablespoons orange blossom water

finely sliced rind of ½ preserved lemon (see page 68)

- Cut the artichoke hearts in half lengthwise, then pull them apart into delicate leaves. Place the clementines on a plate to catch the juice and thinly slice into circles, removing any seeds. Cut into quarters.

- Arrange the artichokes and clementines in a shallow serving bowl. Splash over the orange blossom water and any clementine juice and add the preserved lemon rind. Toss together just before serving.

 ### Artichoke, Egg, and Preserved Lemon Salad

Place 4 prepared fresh or frozen artichoke bottoms and the juice of ½ lemon in a saucepan of boiling water and cook for 10 minutes. Meanwhile, boil 2 eggs in a separate saucepan of boiling water for 6–7 minutes, then drain and refresh under cold running water. Drain and refresh the artichokes, then place upside down to drain. Shell the eggs and cut into quarters. Cut the artichokes into thick slices, then arrange both on a serving dish. Sprinkle with 2–3 teaspoons rinsed and drained baby capers and the finely sliced rind of ½ preserved lemon (see page 68). Mix together 2 tablespoons olive oil, 1 tablespoon cider vinegar, 1 teaspoon honey, 1 crushed garlic clove, and salt and black pepper. Pour the dressing over the salad.

 ### Ginger, Honey, and Preserved Lemon Artichokes

Fill a bowl with cold water and stir in the juice of 1 lemon. Remove the leaves from 4 fresh globe artichokes, cut off the stems, scoop out the choke and all the hairy parts, then trim the bottoms. Put into the water to prevent them from turning brown. Bring a large saucepan of water and ½ teaspoon salt to a boil, then drop in the artichoke bottoms and cook for 10 minutes, until just tender to the point of a knife. Meanwhile, put a pinch of saffron threads into a small bowl, cover with 2 tablespoons water, and set aside. Drain the artichokes, refresh under cold running water, and drain again, then cut into quarters. Heat 2–3 tablespoons olive oil in a heavy saucepan, stir in 2 crushed garlic cloves and ¼ cup peeled and finely chopped fresh ginger root, and cook for 1–2 minutes. Add the saffron water and 1–2 tablespoons honey and stir for 1 minute, then toss in the artichokes, coating them well. Pour in about ½ cup water, season, and sprinkle with the finely sliced rind of 1 preserved lemon (see page 68). Cover and cook gently for 5–10 minutes, turning the artichokes once or twice, until tender. Garnish with a finely chopped small bunch of flat leaf parsley and serve warm or at room temperature.

MOR-STAR-BUN

Beet, Apple, and Orange Blossom Salad

Serves 4

2 beets, peeled and grated

1 crisp green apple, cored
and grated

juice of ½ lemon

2 tablespoons orange blossom
water

salt

- Mix together the beets and apple in a serving bowl.

- Add the lemon juice and orange blossom water and season
with salt. Toss together well and serve.

Beet, Orange, Egg, and Anchovy Salad

Cook 3 eggs in a saucepan of boiling water for 6 minutes. Meanwhile, put 12–16 prepared cooked baby beets into a shallow bowl. Add 1 orange, peeled, cut into quarters, and thinly sliced. Drain the eggs and refresh under cold running water, then shell and cut into quarters. Arrange around the beets and orange. Top with 12 preserved anchovy fillets, rinsed and drained. Dry-fry 2 teaspoons coriander seeds in a small, heavy skillet over medium heat for 2 minutes, until they emit a nutty aroma. Using a mortar and pestle, crush the seeds. Mix together 2 tablespoons olive oil, the juice of 1 lemon, the crushed coriander seeds, 1 teaspoon thyme leaves, and 1 teaspoon honey. Season and pour the dressing over the salad.

Roasted Beet, Orange, and Cinnamon Salad

Put 10 prepared, cooked beets, cut into quarters, 4–6 cardamom pods, and 1–2 teaspoons fennel seeds in an ovenproof dish. Toss with 2 tablespoons olive oil and roast in a preheated oven, at 400°F, for 15 minutes. Meanwhile, using a sharp knife, remove the peel and pith from 2 oranges. Holding the oranges over a bowl to catch the juice, cut down between the membranes and remove the segments. Put into the bowl and set aside. Drizzle 1–2 teaspoons honey over the beets, then return to the oven and cook for another 5–10 minutes. Transfer the beets and all the sweet roasting juices to a bowl. Slip the seeds out of the cardamom pods and add the seeds to the beets, discarding the pods. Toss with 2 tablespoons orange blossom water, season, and add the orange segments and juice. Dust with 1 teaspoon ground cinnamon and serve.

30 Warm Garlicky Lentil Salad

Serves 4

3 tablespoons olive or argan oil
1 red onion, finely chopped
1 teaspoon sugar
2 teaspoons turmeric
1 teaspoon ground cumin
1 teaspoon ground coriander
1 cup brown or green dried lentils,
   rinsed, picked over and drained
about 3½ cups water
3–4 garlic cloves, finely sliced
1 tablespoon brown mustard seeds
juice of 1 lemon
small bunch of cilantro,
   finely chopped
salt and black pepper
lemon wedges, to serve

- Heat 2 tablespoons of the oil in a large, heavy saucepan, stir in the onion and sugar, and cook for 2–3 minutes, until just beginning to brown. Stir in the ground spices, then add the lentils. Pour in the measured water and stir well.

- Bring to a boil, reduce the heat, and simmer for 20 minutes or until the lentils are tender and all the liquid has been absorbed. Transfer the lentils to a shallow serving bowl.

- Heat the remaining oil in a skillet, stir in the garlic and mustard seeds, and cook for 2–3 minutes, until they begin to brown.

- Add to the lentils with the lemon juice and most of the chopped cilantro. Season well and toss until well mixed. Sprinkle with the remaining cilantro and serve warm with lemon wedges to squeeze over the top.

 Lentils with Spicy Garlic Dressing
Place 1¼ cups cooked lentils in a serving bowl. Add 1 large red onion, sliced into bite-size pieces, and a finely chopped small bunch of cilantro. Mix together 2–3 tablespoons olive or argan oil, the juice of 1 lemon, 1–2 seeded and finely chopped red or green chiles, ¼ cup peeled and finely chopped fresh ginger root, 2–3 crushed garlic cloves, and 1 teaspoon honey. Season well with salt and pour the dressing over the lentils. Toss well and serve.

 Garlicky Lentil, Carrot, and Golden Raisin Salad Rinse, pick over, and drain 1 cup brown or green dried lentils, then cook in a saucepan of boiling water for 10–15 minutes or until they are tender but not mushy. Meanwhile, soak 2 tablespoons golden raisins in 2 tablespoons orange blossom water. Drain the lentils, refresh under cold running water, and drain again, then transfer to a serving bowl. Add 4 peeled and shredded carrots, the soaked golden raisins, 1–2 teaspoons caraway seeds, and a small bunch of flat leaf parsley, coarsely chopped. Mix together 2–3 tablespoons olive oil, 2 tablespoons balsamic vinegar, 2 crushed garlic cloves, and 1 teaspoon honey in a bowl and season. Pour the dressing over the salad and toss well.

Spicy Paprika Chickpeas

Serves 4

1 tablespoon ghee or
  clarified butter
1 teaspoon cumin seeds
1 teaspoon coriander seeds
2 garlic cloves, chopped
1½ cups rinsed and drained,
  canned chickpeas
1 teaspoon turmeric
1 teaspoon chili powder
1–2 teaspoons dried thyme
1 teaspoon smoked paprika
salt
flatbread, to serve

- Heat the ghee in a heavy skillet, stir in the cumin seeds, coriander seeds, and garlic and cook for 2–3 minutes, until the garlic begins to brown.

- Toss in the chickpeas and cook for 1–2 minutes, stirring to coat in the spices. Stir in the turmeric and chili powder and cook for another 1–2 minutes, stirring continuously to prevent the spices from burning.

- Sprinkle with the thyme and paprika and season with salt. Transfer to a serving bowl and serve warm with flatbread.

 Chickpea, Sesame, and Paprika Dip

Using a large mortar and pestle, pound 1 (15 oz) can chickpeas, rinsed and drained, 2 garlic cloves, and 1 teaspoon cumin seeds to a coarse paste. Dry-fry 1 tablespoon sesame seeds in a small, heavy skillet over medium heat for 2–3 minutes, until golden brown. Stir most of the seeds into the paste, then mix with 3–4 tablespoons olive oil and the juice of 1 lemon. Season well and spoon into a bowl. Drizzle with a little olive oil, sprinkle the remaining toasted sesame seeds over the dip, and dust with paprika. Serve with strips of toasted pita bread.

 Chickpea Salad with Onion, Eggs, and Paprika Heat 2–3 tablespoons olive oil in a heavy skillet and stir in 1–2 teaspoons cumin seeds and 1 onion, sliced, for 4–5 minutes, until the onions begin to brown. Toss in 1 (15 oz) can chickpeas, rinsed and drained, and cook for 2–3 minutes, then transfer to a bowl. Add 2–3 crushed garlic cloves, the juice of 1 lemon, and 1–2 teaspoons paprika. Season the chickpeas to taste with sea salt and black pepper and toss in a small bunch of flat leaf parsley, coarsely chopped, and a small bunch of mint, coarsely chopped, reserving a little for garnishing. Let the chickpeas cool for 10–15 minutes and season to taste. Heat another 1 tablespoon olive oil in a heavy skillet and crack in 4 eggs. Cook them for 3–4 minutes, until the white is firm, and lift them onto the chickpeas. Sprinkle a little paprika over them and garnish with the reserved herbs.

30 Spicy Sweet Potato and Cilantro Salad

Serves 4

2–3 tablespoons olive or argan oil

1 red onion, coarsely chopped

1 teaspoon cumin seeds

¼ cup peeled and grated fresh
  ginger root

2 orange-fleshed sweet potatoes,
  peeled and cubed

2–3 tablespoons orange
  blossom water

finely sliced or chopped rind of
  1 preserved lemon (see page 68)

small bunch of cilantro,
  finely chopped

8 green olives stuffed with red
  pimento, left whole or halved

salt and black pepper

- Heat the oil in a large, heavy skillet, stir in the onion, cumin seeds, and ginger, and cook for 2–3 minutes. Toss in the sweet potatoes and cook for 1–2 minutes, then pour in just enough water to cover the bottom of the skillet.

- Cover and cook gently for about 10 minutes, until the sweet potatoes are tender but firm and the liquid has been absorbed. Transfer to a shallow bowl, pour the orange blossom water over the potatoes, and let cool.

- Add most of the preserved lemon rind and cilantro to the sweet potatoes, season, and gently toss together. Add the green olives and sprinkle with the remaining preserved lemon and cilantro. Serve at room temperature.

10 Sweet Potato and Cilantro Relish

Peel and grate 2 sweet potatoes and place in a bowl. Pour the juice of 1 lemon over them and stir in the grated rind of 1 small orange and 1 tablespoon finely chopped cilantro. Season well with salt and serve with spicy dishes and syrupy tagines.

20 Sautéed Cilantro Sweet Potatoes

Peel and cube 2 sweet potatoes. Steam for 10 minutes, until just tender. Heat 1–2 tablespoons olive or argan oil or 1 tablespoon ghee or clarified butter in a heavy skillet, stir in 2 finely chopped garlic cloves, 1 seeded and finely chopped green or red chile, 1 tablespoon peeled and finely chopped fresh ginger root, 2 teaspoons coriander seeds, and 1 teaspoon sugar and cook for 2–3 minutes. Add the steamed sweet potato and cook, stirring, for another 2–3 minutes. Season and sprinkle with a finely chopped small bunch of cilantro. Mix together ¼–⅓ cup plain yogurt, 1 crushed garlic clove, and salt and black pepper in a bowl and serve with the sweet potatoes.

30 Roasted Zucchini, Apple, and Clementine Salad

Serves 4–6

2 zucchini, halved and thinly
 sliced lengthwise
1 crisp green or red apple, such
 as Pippin, Rome, or Jonagold,
 cored and thinly sliced
2–3 tablespoons olive oil
1 tablespoon honey
2 teaspoons fennel seeds
2 sweet clementines,
 peeled and pith removed
juice of 1 lemon
finely sliced rind of ½ preserved
 lemon (see page 68)
salt

- Put the zucchini and apple into a baking dish and spoon the oil over them. Put into a preheated oven, at 400°F, for about 15 minutes. Drizzle with the honey, then return to the oven and cook for another 5–10 minutes, until softened and slightly browned.

- Meanwhile, dry-fry the fennel seeds in a small, heavy skillet over medium heat for 2–3 minutes, until they emit a nutty aroma. Set aside.

- Place the clementines on a plate to catch the juice and thinly slice into circles, removing any seeds. Arrange the slices in a serving dish and spoon the roasted zucchini and apple on top.

- Stir any clementine juice into the roasting juices in the baking dish. Add the lemon juice and season with a little salt. Drizzle the dressing over the salad and sprinkle with the toasted fennel seeds and preserved lemon rind. Serve warm or at room temperature.

Baby Zucchini and Apple with Dukkah

Dip Mix together 2 tablespoons prepared dukkah spice mix, 2 crushed garlic cloves, 1 finely chopped red chile, 2 tablespoons olive oil, the juice of 1 lemon, and a finely chopped small bunch of cilantro in a small bowl. Season with salt and serve with 4 halved baby zucchini and 1 cored apple, cut into segments, for dipping.

 Zucchini, Apple, and Lime Salad

Place 2 thinly sliced zucchini and 1 cored and thinly sliced green apple in a bowl. Pour in the juice of 1 lime. Remove the rind from another lime and, using a sharp knife, cut down between the membranes and remove the segments, then add them to the bowl. Sprinkle with 1 scant teaspoon sugar, season with salt, and add 1–2 tablespoons finely shredded mint leaves. Toss well, garnish with a little more shredded mint, and serve.

Chargrilled Bell Peppers with Feta

Serves 4

3 red, green, or yellow
   bell peppers
1⅔ cups crumbled goat
   or feta cheese
1 red onion, finely chopped
small bunch of parsley,
   finely chopped
finely chopped or shredded
   rind of 1 preserved lemon
   (see page 68)
1–2 tablespoons argan or olive oil
flatbread, to serve

- Place the bell peppers directly over a gas flame or under a preheated hot broiler for 10–15 minutes, turning occasionally, until buckled and charred. Place in a plastic food bag to sweat for 2–3 minutes, then hold by the stems under cold running water and carefully peel off the skins. Put onto a board, remove the stems and seeds, then finely slice the flesh.

- Transfer the chargrilled peppers to a shallow bowl and sprinkle with the crumbled cheese.

- In a separate bowl, mix together the onion, parsley, and preserved lemon rind, then sprinkle the mixture over the peppers. Drizzle with the oil and serve with flatbread.

1 Pickled Green Peppers

Wash 8 long green Mediterranean peppers and pat dry, then tightly pack into a large sterilized jar. Mix together 1¼ cups water, 1¼ cups white wine vinegar, and 1 scant tablespoon salt, then pour the mixture over the peppers, making sure they are submerged; add more vinegar, if necessary. Tightly seal with a vinegar-proof lid and store in the refrigerator for at least 2 weeks before using. (The peppers can be stored in the refrigerator for 4–6 weeks.)

2 Red Pepper Paste

Seed and chop 2 long red Mediterranean peppers and 2 red chiles, put into a food processor with 1–2 tablespoons olive oil, 1 tablespoon sugar, 1 teaspoon fennel seeds, 1 teaspoon sea salt, and a splash of balsamic vinegar and process together. Transfer the mixture to a heavy skillet and heat until bubbling, stirring continuously. Reduce the heat and simmer for about 15 minutes, until thick. Serve as a warm dip or use as a condiment or sauce. (The cooled paste can be stored in a sealed sterilized jar in the refrigerator for 1–2 weeks.)

 Pear, Endive, and Rose Petal Salad

Serves 4

2 ripe but firm pears, peeled, cored, and thinly sliced

juice of ½ lemon

1–2 tablespoons rose water

2 heads of white or red endive, leaves separated and rinsed

1 tablespoon olive oil

1 teaspoon honey

small handful of fresh, scented rose petals

salt

- Put the pears into a bowl and lightly toss with the lemon juice and rose water. Let stand for 5 minutes.

- Arrange the endive leaves in a shallow salad bowl. Remove the pear from the rose water and lemon juice with a slotted spoon and sprinkle the pear over and around the endive.

- Mix the oil with any rose water and lemon juice left in the bowl and pour the dressing over the salad. Drizzle with the honey and sprinkle with salt. Sprinkle with the rose petals and toss just before serving.

 Endive, Peach, and Rose Water Salad

Trim 2 heads of red or white endive, separate the leaves, then rinse and drain. Peel, halve, and pit 2 ripe but firm peaches. Slice each half into 4 segments. Arrange the endive leaves and peach slices in a shallow dish. Sprinkle with the finely sliced rind of ½ preserved lemon (see page 68) and pour 2 tablespoons rose water over the salad. Toss gently just before serving.

 Pickled Pears with Rose Petals

Put ½ cup water, 1¼ cups white wine or cider vinegar, 2 tablespoons honey, 2 cinnamon sticks, 6–8 allspice berries, and a pinch of saffron threads in a heavy saucepan and bring to a boil, stirring continuously until the honey has dissolved. Peel 4 pears, keeping the stems intact, halve lengthwise, and add to the pan. Bring back to a boil, then reduce the heat and poach gently for 15–20 minutes, until tender but still firm. Remove the pears and place in a sterilized jar. Pour the hot liquid over them and let cool. Seal with a vinegar-proof lid and store in the refrigerator for 2–3 weeks before using. Serve garnished with fresh rose petals. (The pickled pears can be stored in the refrigerator for 4–6 weeks.)

30 Apricot and Apple Chutney with Pan-Fried Cheese

Serves 4

1¾ cups chopped dried apricots

1 tart green apple, peeled, cored, and chopped

1 onion, finely chopped

2–3 garlic cloves, finely chopped

1 tablespoon peeled and grated fresh ginger root

1 tablespoon golden raisins

2 cinnamon sticks

grated rind and juice of 1 lemon

²⁄₃ cup white wine vinegar

pinch of chili powder

²⁄₃ cup granulated sugar

1 tablespoon honey

2–3 tablespoons orange blossom water

2–3 tablespoons sunflower oil

8 oz Muenster or haloumi cheese, thickly sliced

salt

- To make the chutney, put the apricots, apple, onion, garlic, ginger, golden raisins, cinnamon, lemon rind and juice, vinegar, chili powder, and sugar into a heavy saucepan and bring to a boil, stirring continuously, then cook over medium heat for 20 minutes, stirring occasionally, until thick.

- Add the honey and orange blossom water and cook gently for another 5–10 minutes, until thick and fragrant, then season with salt.

- Meanwhile, heat the oil in a heavy skillet, add the cheese, and cook for 3–4 minutes, turning once, until golden brown. Drain on paper towels. Serve immediately with the chutney.

 10 Apricot and Apple Yogurt Dip

Peel, core, and thinly slice or grate 1 crisp apple and toss with the juice of ½ lemon. In a separate bowl, beat together ⅓–½ cup thick, plain yogurt and 2 crushed garlic cloves and season. Fold 1 cup thin dried apricot strips and the apple into the yogurt and serve with chunks of warm crusty bread.

 20 Apricot, Apple, and Almond Salad

Put 1¼ cups whole almonds in a bowl, pour enough boiling water over them to just cover, then let soak for 5–10 minutes. Meanwhile, put 1⅓ cups thin dried apricot strips and 1 cored crisp apple, sliced into thin strips, into a separate bowl. Pour in the juice of 1 lemon and 2 tablespoons orange blossom water and toss well. Drain and rinse the almonds, then rub off the skins with your fingers. Slice the almonds into thin sticks and toss with the apricots and apple.

30 Warm Stuffed Dates with Spiced Syrup

Serves 4

12 soft pitted dates

12 walnut halves

1–2 tablespoons ghee or
clarified butter

2 tablespoons pomegranate syrup

2 tablespoons granulated sugar

1 cinnamon stick

seeds of 4 cardamom pods

2–3 cloves

2–3 tablespoons orange
blossom water

salt

small bunch of flat leaf parsley,
finely chopped, to garnish

- Find the opening in each pitted date and stuff it with a walnut half.

- Melt the ghee in a heavy skillet, add the stuffed dates, and cook for 2–3 minutes, turning occasionally. Stir in the pomegranate syrup, sugar, spices, and enough water to just cover the bottom of the skillet. Splash in the orange blossom water and heat until bubbling. Reduce the heat, cover, and simmer for about 15 minutes.

- Remove the lid and simmer for another 5 minutes, adding a little more orange blossom water, if necessary. Season with salt and transfer the stuffed dates to a serving dish. Drizzle with the syrupy juice, garnish with the parsley, and serve hot or at room temperature.

---

10 Pickled Fresh Dates

Pack 10 pitted fresh dates into a sterilized jar. Put 1¼ cups cider vinegar, 2 tablespoons packed light brown sugar, 2 cinnamon sticks, 2 dried red chiles, and the seeds of 4–6 cardamom pods in a heavy saucepan and bring to a boil, stirring continuously. Reduce the heat and simmer for about 8 minutes. Pour the mixture over the dates, seal with a vinegar-proof lid, and let cool. Store in the refrigerator for 1–2 weeks before using. (The pickled dates can be stored in the refrigerator for 3–4 weeks.)

20 Date Relish

Heat 1 tablespoon olive oil in a skillet, stir in 1 finely chopped red onion, 2 finely chopped garlic cloves, and 1 teaspoon cumin seeds, and cook for 2–3 minutes, until the onion begins to brown. Toss in 3 tablespoons finely chopped pitted dates, 2 teaspoons finely chopped Pickled Red Chiles (see page 70), and 1–2 teaspoons packed light brown sugar and cook for another 2–3 minutes. Stir in ¼ cup pomegranate syrup and cook the mixture gently for another 2–3 minutes. Season with salt, toss in 2 tablespoons fresh pomegranate seeds, and let cool. Serve with toasted flatbreads or cheese.

30 Mixed Pickled Vegetables

Serves 4

1 small cucumber

1 teaspoon salt

2 carrots, peeled

1 large white radish, peeled

1 red bell pepper, cored
  and seeded

2 tablespoons blanched almonds

2 teaspoons pink peppercorns

1–2 teaspoons cumin seeds

pinch of saffron threads

1–2 cinnamon sticks

juice of 2 lemons

1–2 tablespoons cider vinegar

1 tablespoon granulated sugar

1–2 tablespoons orange
  blossom water

2 tablespoons finely chopped
  cilantro

- Peel and seed the cucumber, then cut into matchsticks and put into a colander, sprinkle with the salt, and let stand for 5 minutes. Rinse, drain, and pat dry, then put into a large, nonmetallic bowl.

- Cut the carrots, radish, and red bell pepper into matchsticks. Add to the cucumber with the almonds and spices, then stir in the lemon juice, vinegar, sugar, and orange blossom water. Cover and chill for 15–20 minutes. Just before serving, toss in the cilantro.

- (The pickles can also be stored in a sterilized jar, sealed with a vinegar-proof lid, in the refrigerator for 3–4 weeks.)

 Pickled Purple Turnips

Trim and peel 8 small white turnips, then rinse and pat dry. Pack into a sterilized jar with 4 peeled garlic cloves and 2 slices of raw beet. Mix together 1¼ cups white wine vinegar, 1¼ cups water, and 1 teaspoon sea salt, then pour the mixture over the turnips. Seal with a vinegar-proof lid and store in the refrigerator for 1–2 weeks, until the turnips have taken on a purplish pink hue. (The pickles can be stored in the refrigerator for 3–4 weeks.)

 Pickled Stuffed Cabbage Leaves

Put 8 green cabbage leaves in a steamer and cook for 5–6 minutes, until softened. Refresh under cold running water and drain well. Place the leaves on a flat surface and remove the central ribs so that the leaves lie flat. Using a mortar and pestle, pound 3 garlic cloves and 3 tablespoons walnuts to a coarse paste. Stir in 1 finely chopped red chile and 2 teaspoons finely chopped preserved lemon rind (see page 68). Mix with 1 tablespoon olive oil, then place a teaspoonful of the mixture near the top of each leaf. Pull the top edge over the mixture, tuck in the sides, and roll the leaf into a tight log. Tightly pack the stuffed leaves into a nonmetallic bowl or sterilized jar and pour 1¼ cups white wine or cider vinegar combined with a little salt over them. Cover the bowl or jar and store in the refrigerator for 1–2 weeks before use. (The pickled stuffed cabbage leaves can be stored in the refrigerator for 3–4 weeks.)

20 Preserved Lemons

Serves 4

8–10 organic unwaxed lemons,
    washed and dried
about ⅔ cup sea salt
juice of 3–4 lemons

- Slice the ends off each lemon and stand them on one end. Using a small, sharp knife, carefully make 2 vertical cuts three-quarters of the way through each lemon, as if cutting into quarters, but keep the bottoms intact. Stuff 1 tablespoon of the salt into each lemon, then pack into a large sterilized jar and seal tightly. Store in the refrigerator for 3–4 days to soften the skins.

- Press the lemons down into the jar until tightly packed, then cover with the lemon juice. Seal the jar and store in the refrigerator for at least 1 month before use. Keep in the refrigerator for 3–4 months.

- To use, rinse off the salt and pat dry with paper towels. Cut the lemon into quarters and, using a small, sharp knife, remove the flesh, seeds, and pith. Finely slice or chop the rind and use as required.

10 Pickled Lemons

Pack 8–10 small unwaxed lemons into a sterilized jar. Put 2½ cups white wine vinegar, 2–3 tablespoons granulated sugar, 1 tablespoon coriander seeds, 2 dried sage sprigs, and 2–3 dried red chiles in a small, heavy saucepan and bring to a boil, stirring constantly until the sugar has dissolved, then reduce the heat and simmer for 5 minutes. Pour the mixture over the lemons, seal with a vinegar-proof lid, and let cool. Store in the refrigerator for 2 weeks before using. (The pickled lemons can also be stored in the refrigerator for 4–6 weeks.)

30 Lemon and Herb Jam

Peel and finely shred the rind of 4 unwaxed lemons, then halve the flesh and squeeze the juice. Put the rind into a small, heavy saucepan with 1 tablespoon peeled and finely chopped fresh ginger root, 1 teaspoon coriander seeds, and 1 teaspoon finely chopped dried red chile. Add the lemon juice, ⅓ cup cider vinegar, and 2 tablespoons granulated sugar, then heat until bubbling, stirring continuously until the sugar has dissolved. Reduce the heat and simmer for 15–20 minutes, until the mixture is almost dry, making sure the sugar doesn't burn. Season with a little salt and let cool in the pan. Toss in 1 tablespoon each of finely chopped cilantro and mint and serve with bread and cheese.

Serves 4 (a little goes a long way)

12 large fresh red chiles, such as Guajillo, Mexican Horn, or New Mexico
3 tablespoons olive oil
1 teaspoon cumin seed
1 teaspoon coriander seeds
1 teaspoon caraway or fennel seeds
3–4 garlic cloves, chopped
1 teaspoon sea salt
1 tablespoon finely chopped cilantro
vegetable sticks or toasted flatbreads, to serve

- Put the chiles in an ovenproof dish, pour the oil over them, and roast in a preheated oven, at 400°F, for 20–25 minutes, until the skins begin to buckle. Meanwhile, dry-fry all the seeds in a small, heavy skillet over medium heat for 2–3 minutes, until they emit a nutty aroma, then grind in a spice grinder.

- Using a small, sharp knife, remove the stems and skins from the roasted chiles. Slit lengthwise and scrape out the seeds. Using a mortar and pestle, pound the chile flesh, garlic, and salt to a smooth paste. Add the spices, mix with 2–3 tablespoons of the roasting oil, and stir in the cilantro.

- Spoon the harissa into a small bowl, drizzle with a little more roasting oil, and serve with vegetable sticks or toasted flatbread. Alternatively, put into a sterilized jar, top with a thin layer of olive oil, and seal. (The harissa paste can also be stored in the refrigerator for up to 4 weeks.)

---

1 Pickled Red Chiles
Using a small, sharp knife, slit 8 red Guajillo or Serrano chiles lengthwise, without cutting right through, and pack into a sterilized jar. Put 1¾ cups white wine vinegar, 2 tablespoons granulated sugar, and 2 teaspoons each of sea salt and coriander seeds in a saucepan and bring to a boil, stirring until the sugar has dissolved. Pour the mixture over the chiles to cover, seal with a vinegar-proof lid, and let cool. Store in the refrigerator for at least 2 weeks before using. (The chiles can be stored in the refrigerator for 4–6 weeks.)

2 Spiced Dukkah Dip
Dry-fry 1 tablespoon dried red pepper flakes in a heavy skillet over medium heat for 2 minutes, then remove and set aside. Using the same skillet, dry-fry 2 tablespoons each of hazelnuts and sunflower seeds, 1 tablespoon sesame seeds, and 2 teaspoons each of cumin seeds and coriander seeds for 2–3 minutes, until they emit a nutty aroma. Using a mortar and pestle, pound the nuts and seeds with 1 teaspoon sea salt to a paste. Heat 2 tablespoons olive oil in the skillet, stir in 2 crushed garlic cloves and the dried red pepper flakes, and cook for 2 minutes, until the garlic begins to brown. Stir the oil into the nut mixture and mix well, then stir in the juice of ½ lemon. Spoon into a bowl and let stand for 10 minutes to let the flavors mingle. Serve with toasted flatbreads or vegetable sticks.

QuickCook

Soups, Pastries, and Savory Snacks

Recipes listed by cooking time

30

20

30 Honeyed Pumpkin and Ginger Broth

Serves 4

2 tablespoons olive oil

1 tablespoon butter

1 onion, finely chopped

½ cup fresh peeled and finely chopped ginger root

2 dried red chiles

2–3 celery sticks, cut into bite-size pieces

6 cups peeled and seeded pumpkin or butternut squash bite-size chunks

4 cups hot chicken or vegetable stock

small bunch of flat leaf parsley, finely chopped

1–2 tablespoons honey

salt and black pepper

- Heat the oil and butter in a large, heavy saucepan, stir in the onion and ginger, and cook for 2–3 minutes, until they begin to brown. Add the chiles, celery, and pumpkin and cook for 1–2 minutes, stirring to coat well.

- Pour in the stock and bring to a boil, then reduce the heat and cook gently for 20–25 minutes, until the vegetables are tender. Season and stir in most of the parsley.

- Meanwhile, in a small saucepan, gently heat the honey until it begins to simmer. Ladle the broth into serving bowls, drizzle the hot honey over it, and garnish with the remaining parsley.

 **Pumpkin and Ginger Butter Dip**

Melt 4 tablespoons butter in a heavy saucepan, stir in ¼ cup peeled and grated fresh ginger root, and cook over low heat for 1–2 minutes. Stir in 2⅔ cups canned pumpkin puree and cook for 2 minutes, until heated through, then season. Serve with chunks of crusty bread.

 Pureed Pumpkin and Ginger Soup

Heat 2 tablespoons olive oil and a pat of butter in a heavy saucepan, stir in 1 chopped onion, ¼ cup peeled and chopped fresh ginger root, 1 teaspoon coriander seeds, 1 teaspoon fennel seeds, and 1 teaspoon sugar, and cook for 1–2 minutes. Add 9 cups peeled, seeded, and diced pumpkin or butternut squash and cook for 1 minute, stirring to coat. Pour in 5 cups hot chicken or vegetable stock and bring to a boil, then cook over medium heat for 15 minutes, until the pumpkin is tender. Puree the soup with an immersion blender or process in a blender, then return to the heat and season well. Swirl in ½ cup light cream and serve with chunks of crusty bread.

30 Tomato, Ras el Hanout, and Vermicelli Soup

Serves 4

8 large ripe tomatoes
2–3 tablespoons olive or argan oil
4 cloves
2 onions, chopped
2 celery sticks, chopped
1 carrot, peeled and chopped
1–2 teaspoons sugar
1 tablespoon tomato paste
1–2 teaspoons ras el hanout
large bunch of cilantro,
    finely chopped
6 cups hot vegetable stock
4 oz fine vermicelli, broken into
    small pieces
salt and black pepper
chunks of crusty bread, to serve
    (optional)

- Put the tomatoes into a heatproof bowl and pour enough boiling water over them to cover. Let stand for 1–2 minutes, then drain, cut a cross at the stem end of each tomato, and peel off the skins. Coarsely chop and set aside.

- Meanwhile, heat the oil in a heavy saucepan, stir in the cloves, onions, celery, and carrot, and cook for 3–4 minutes, until they begin to brown. Add the tomatoes and sugar and cook over medium heat for 4–5 minutes, until the mixture is thick.

- Stir in the tomato paste, ras el hanout, and most of the cilantro. Pour in the stock and bring to a boil, then cook over medium heat for 15 minutes. Stir in the vermicelli, season, and cook for another 5–6 minutes, until the pasta is just tender.

- Garnish with the remaining cilantro and ladle into serving bowls. Serve with crusty bread, if desired.

 Quick Tomato and Ras el Hanout Pasta
Heat 1 tablespoon olive oil and a pat of butter in a heavy saucepan, stir in 1 crushed garlic clove and 1 teaspoon crushed coriander seeds, and cook for 1–2 minutes. Stir in 1–2 teaspoons ras el hanout and 1 teaspoon sugar, add 1⅔ cups tomato puree or sauce and cook over low heat for 6–8 minutes. Season with salt and black pepper and swirl in 1 tablespoon olive oil with a finely chopped small bunch of cilantro. Serve the sauce spooned over cooked fresh pasta.

 Pureed Tomato and Ras el Hanout Soup Heat 2 tablespoons olive oil and a pat of butter in a heavy saucepan, add 2 chopped onions and 1 teaspoon sugar, and cook, stirring, for 2–3 minutes, until the onions are soft and begin to colour. Stir in 2 teaspoons tomato paste and 2 teaspoons ras el hanout, add 1 (14½ oz) can diced tomatoes and 3¾ cups hot vegetable stock, and bring to a boil, then cook over medium heat for 10 minutes. Puree the soup with an immersion blender or process in a blender. Return to the heat and season to taste. Garnish with a little finely chopped cilantro and serve with crusty bread.

MOR-SOUP-FAX

10

20 Lamb, Chickpea, and Cinnamon Broth

Serves 4

2 tablespoons ghee, clarified
  butter, or argan oil
1 onion, finely chopped
1 garlic clove, finely chopped
1 teaspoon coriander seeds
1 teaspoon cumin seeds
2 dried red chiles
2–3 cinnamon sticks
8 oz lean lamb, cut into thin strips
1 (15 oz) can chickpeas, rinsed
  and drained
5 cups hot lamb or chicken stock
small bunch of flat leaf parsley,
  coarsely chopped
salt and black pepper
lemon wedges, to serve (optional)

- Heat the ghee, clarified butter, or oil in a heavy saucepan, stir in the onion, garlic, and spices, and cook for 2–3 minutes, until the onion begins to brown.

- Add the lamb and cook for 1–2 minutes, stirring to coat well, then add the chickpeas. Pour in the stock and bring to a boil, then cook over medium heat for 15 minutes.

- Stir in the parsley and season. Serve the broth with lemon wedges to squeeze over the top, if desired.

---

10 Quick Chickpea and Cinnamon Sauce Put 1 (15 oz) can chickpeas, rinsed and drained, 2 crushed garlic cloves, and 1 teaspoon cumin seeds into a food processor and process to a thick puree. Melt 1 tablespoon butter in a heavy saucepan, stir in 1 cup heavy cream, a pinch of freshly grated nutmeg, and 1 teaspoon ground cinnamon, and bring to a boil, then remove from the heat and gently beat in the chickpea puree. Season, dust with a little cinnamon, and serve with lamb.

30 Cinnamon Lamb, Chickpea, and Tomato Soup Heat 2 tablespoons ghee or clarified butter in a large, heavy saucepan, stir in 1 finely chopped onion, 1 diced celery stick, and 2 peeled and diced small carrots, and cook for 3–4 minutes, until they begin to brown. Add 2–3 crushed garlic cloves, 1 teaspoon cumin seeds, and 8 oz diced lamb, and cook for 2–3 minutes, until lightly browned. Stir in 2 teaspoons turmeric, 1–2 teaspoons paprika, 2 teaspoons ground cinnamon, 1–2 teaspoons sugar, and 2 bay leaves, then add 1 tablespoon tomato paste, 1 (14½ oz) can diced tomatoes, drained of juice, and 1 (15 oz) can chickpeas, rinsed and drained. Pour in 6 cups hot lamb or chicken stock and bring to a boil, then cook over medium heat for 20 minutes. Season and stir in a coarsely chopped small bunch each of flat leaf parsley and cilantro. Serve with lemon wedges to squeeze over the soup.

3⓪ Lemony Beef, Bean, and Cumin Soup

Serves 4

2 tablespoons ghee, smen, clarified butter, or argan oil

1 onion, finely chopped

2–3 garlic cloves, finely chopped

2 teaspoons cumin seeds

1 teaspoon sugar

8 oz lean beef, diced

2 dried red chiles

2 teaspoons turmeric

6 cups hot beef stock

1 (15 oz) can kidney or fava beans, rinsed and drained

juice of 1 lemon

large bunch of flat leaf parsley, finely chopped

salt and black pepper

lemon wedges, to serve

- Heat the ghee, smen, clarified butter, or oil in a large, heavy saucepan, stir in the onion, garlic, cumin seeds, and sugar, and cook for 2–3 minutes, until the onion begins to brown.

- Add the beef and cook for 1 minute, stirring to coat well, then add the chiles and turmeric. Pour in the stock and bring to a boil, then cook over medium heat for 15 minutes.

- Stir in the beans, lemon juice, and most of the parsley, reduce the heat, and cook for another 10 minutes. Season, garnish with the remaining parsley, and serve with lemon wedges to squeeze over the soup.

 1⓪ Cumin and Lemon Beef and Beans Heat 2 tablespoons ghee in a saucepan, stir in 1 chopped onion, 2 chopped garlic cloves, 2 teaspoons cumin seeds, and 1 teaspoon sugar. Cook for 2–3 minutes. Toss in 4 slices of cooked beef, cut into strips, and cook for 1–2 minutes. Add 2 cups rinsed and drained, canned mixed beans (kidney beans, pinto beans, chickpeas), and cook for 1 minute. Pour in the juice of 1 lemon, cook for 3–4 minutes, season, and stir in a finely chopped small bunch of flat leaf parsley. Serve on toasted flatbreads with dollops of yogurt.

 2⓪ Beef and Cumin Seed Broth with Lemon Heat 1 tablespoon ghee, smen, clarified butter, or argan oil in a heavy saucepan, stir in 1 finely chopped onion, 2 finely chopped garlic cloves, 1 teaspoon cumin seeds, and 1 teaspoon sugar, and cook for 2–3 minutes. Add 12 oz lean beef, cut into thin strips, and cook for 1 minute, stirring to coat well. Add 1 teaspoon turmeric, 1–2 dried red chiles, and a bunch of parsley leaves. Pour in 5 cups hot beef or chicken stock and bring to a boil, then cook over medium heat for 15 minutes. Season to taste. Meanwhile, melt 1 tablespoon ghee in a small skillet, add 1 teaspoon cumin seeds, and cook, stirring, for 1–2 minutes, then swirl it into the broth. Garnish with a finely chopped small bunch of flat leaf parsley and serve with lemon wedges to squeeze over the broth.

3⬤ Fino, Harissa, and Roasted Pepper Fish Soup

Serves 4

2 red, orange, or yellow
  bell peppers
2 tablespoons olive or argan oil
1 onion, finely chopped
2 garlic cloves, finely chopped
1–2 teaspoons harissa paste
  (see page 70)
small bunch of flat leaf parsley,
  finely chopped
4 cups hot fish stock
⅔ cup fino sherry or white wine
1 (14½ oz) can diced tomatoes,
  drained of juice
2 lb firm-fleshed fish, such as
  sea bass, halibut, or red snapper
  skinned and cut into chunks
salt and black pepper
small bunch of cilantro, finely
  chopped, to garnish
crusty bread, to serve

- Place the bell peppers directly over a gas flame or under a preheated hot broiler for 4–5 minutes, turning occasionally with tongs, until the skin is charred in places. Place in a plastic food bag to sweat for 5 minutes, then hold by the stems under cold running water and carefully peel off the skins. Place on a board, remove the stems and seeds, then cut into thick strips. Set aside.

- Meanwhile, heat the oil in a large, heavy saucepan, add the onion and garlic, and cook for 2–3 minutes, until they begin to brown. Add the harissa and parsley and pour in the stock. Bring to a boil, then reduce the heat and simmer for 10 minutes.

- Add the sherry or wine and tomatoes, then gently stir in the fish pieces and chargrilled peppers. Increase the heat and bring to a boil, then reduce the heat and simmer for 5–6 minutes, or until the fish is cooked through. Season, garnish with the cilantro, and serve with crusty bread.

 Harissa Fish Stock Couscous

Put 1–1½ lb heads, tails, bones, and scrap pieces of fish in a saucepan. Add 2 smashed garlic cloves, 1 quartered onion, 4–6 black peppercorns, a bunch of flat leaf parsley leaves and stems, 1 teaspoon sea salt, and 1 teaspoon harissa paste (see page 70). Add 5 cups boiling water and boil for 8–10 minutes. Strain, spoon over couscous, and garnish with a finely chopped small bunch of cilantro.

 Fino and Harissa Fish Broth

Heat 1–2 tablespoons olive oil in a heavy saucepan, add 1 finely chopped onion, 2 finely chopped garlic cloves, and 1 teaspoon sugar, and cook for 2–3 minutes, until the onion begins to brown. Stir in 1–2 teaspoons harissa paste (see page 70), 1 (14½ oz) can diced tomatoes, drained of juice, 4 cups hot fish stock, and ⅔ cup fino sherry and bring to a boil, then cook over medium heat for 10 minutes. Add 1½ lb firm white fish, such as halibut or red snapper, skinned and cut into chunks, and simmer gently for 5–6 minutes, or until cooked through. Season to taste, garnish with a finely chopped small bunch of cilantro, and serve with couscous or chunks of crusty bread.

 # Mussel, Chile, and Cilantro Broth

Serves 4

2 tablespoons olive oil
1 onion, finely chopped
2 garlic cloves, finely chopped
2 red chiles, seeded and
  finely chopped
1–2 teaspoons turmeric
3½ cups hot fish or shellfish stock
1¼ cups white wine
2¼ lb fresh mussels
small bunch of flat leaf parsley,
  finely chopped
small bunch of cilantro,
  finely chopped
salt and black pepper
chunks of crusty bread,
  to serve (optional)

- Heat the oil in a heavy saucepan, add the onion, garlic, and chiles, and cook for 2–3 minutes. Stir in the turmeric, then pour in the stock and white wine. Bring to a boil, then reduce the heat and cook gently for 8–10 minutes.

- Meanwhile, scrub the mussels in plenty of cold water. Scrape off any barnacles and beards with a knife and discard any mussels that fail to open when lightly tapped on a work surface. Rinse well, then drain.

- Season the broth, then add the mussels with half the herbs and bring to a boil. Cover and cook gently for 5 minutes, or until the mussels open. Discard any that remain shut. Sprinkle with the remaining herbs and serve with crusty bread, if desired.

 Chile and Cilantro Mussel Stock

Couscous Put 2¼ lb fresh mussels, prepared as above, into a large saucepan. Add 1 quartered onion, 2 smashed garlic cloves, 2 dried red chiles, and a bunch of cilantro leaves and stems. Pour in enough water to cover the contents, cover with a lid, and bring to a boil, then cook for 6–8 minutes or until the mussels open. Discard any that remain shut. Season and spoon the stock over couscous.

 Creamy Chile and Cilantro Mussel

Broth Heat 2 tablespoons olive oil in a large, heavy saucepan, add 1 finely chopped onion, 2 finely chopped garlic cloves, and 2 seeded and finely chopped red chiles, and cook for 2–3 minutes. Add 2 teaspoons turmeric and 2 fresh or dried bay leaves, then pour in 3½ cups hot fish stock and 1¼ cups white wine. Bring to a boil, then reduce the heat and simmer for 10 minutes. Meanwhile, prepare 3 lb fresh mussels as above. Add to the pan, cover, and simmer for another 5 minutes or until the mussels open. Strain the liquid through a colander into a separate saucepan and simmer over low heat. Shell the mussels, discarding the shells and any that have remained shut. Add the mussels to the broth, stir in ⅔ cup heavy cream and a finely chopped small bunch of cilantro, and season. Garnish with a little more finely chopped cilantro and serve with couscous or chunks of crusty bread.

3 Minty Chicken and Rice Soup

Serves 4

2 tablespoons olive or argan oil

2 onions, finely chopped

1 red chile, seeded and
finely chopped

1 teaspoon coriander seeds

2 teaspoons dried mint

10 oz skinless, boneless chicken
breasts, cut into thin strips

½ cup medium grain white rice,
such as paella or risotto,
rinsed and drained

2 teaspoons tomato paste

1 teaspoon sugar

6 cups hot chicken stock

salt and black pepper

small bunch of mint, finely
shredded, to garnish

lemon wedges, to serve (optional)

- Heat the oil in a heavy saucepan, stir in the onions, chile, and coriander seeds, and cook for 2–3 minutes. Add the dried mint and chicken and cook for 2 minutes, stirring to coat well.

- Stir in the rice, then add the tomato paste, sugar, and stock. Bring to a boil, then reduce the heat and simmer for 20–25 minutes, until cooked through.

- Season, garnish with the shredded mint, and serve with lemon wedges to squeeze over the soup, if desired.

 1 **Quick Chicken and Mint Stock Couscous** In a small saucepan, stir 1 chicken bouillon cube into 2½ cups boiling water until it dissolves. Add the juice of 1 lemon, 2 dried red chiles, and a large bunch of mint leaves. Bring to a boil and cook over medium heat for 5–6 minutes. Season and spoon over couscous.

 2 **Chicken and Mint Broth** Heat 1 tablespoon olive oil in a heavy saucepan, add 1 finely chopped onion, 2 finely chopped garlic cloves, 1 seeded and chopped green chile, and 1 teaspoon coriander seeds, and cook for 1–2 minutes. Stir in 2 teaspoons dried mint and 10 oz thinly sliced skinless, boneless chicken breasts and cook for 1–2 minutes. Pour in 4 cups hot chicken stock and bring to a boil, then cook over medium heat for 15 minutes, until cooked through. Season and stir in a finely chopped small bunch of mint. Serve with lemon wedges to squeeze over the broth.

10 Simple Herb, Chile, and Saffron Broth

Serves 4

3½ cups boiling water
2–3 dried red chiles
2 teaspoons cumin seeds
1 teaspoon coriander seeds
1 teaspoon saffron threads
small bunch of flat leaf parsley
  leaves and stems
small bunch of cilantro leaves
  and stems
small bunch of mint leaves
4–6 peppercorns
1 teaspoon sea salt

- Pour the measured water into a saucepan set over medium heat. Add the remaining ingredients and boil gently for 8–10 minutes.

- Strain and serve between courses or as a digestive.

Herbed Vegetable Soup with Chiles

Heat 2 tablespoons olive oil in a heavy saucepan, add 1 chopped onion, 2 chopped garlic cloves, and 1 teaspoon each of coriander seeds and cumin seeds, and cook for 1–2 minutes. Stir in 2 diced celery sticks, 2 peeled and diced carrots, 3 peeled and diced potatoes, and 3½ cups hot chicken or vegetable stock and bring to a boil. Add 1 (6 oz) package baby spinach leaves and a bunch of flat leaf parsley leaves and stems, then cook over medium heat for 12–15 minutes. Puree with an immersion blender or process in a blender. Return to the heat and season. Serve garnished with 1–2 seeded and finely chopped red or green chiles.

Herb, Chile, and Saffron Vegetable Soup

Soup Heat 2 tablespoons olive or argan oil in a heavy saucepan, add 2 finely chopped onions, 2 finely chopped garlic cloves, 2 seeded and finely chopped red or green chiles, and 1 teaspoon each of cumin seeds and coriander seeds, and cook for 2–3 minutes. Add 2 diced celery sticks, 2 peeled and diced carrots, and 4 peeled and diced new potatoes, then cover and cook for 2–3 minutes. Stir in 2 diced zucchini, a pinch of saffron threads, and 6 cups hot vegetable or chicken stock. Bring to a boil, then reduce the heat and cook gently for 20 minutes. Season and stir in a finely chopped small bunch each of flat leaf parsley, cilantro, and mint leaves and a few finely chopped dill sprigs. Garnish with a little more finely chopped dill and serve with lemon wedges to squeeze over the soup.

Carrot, Cilantro, and Lentil Soup

Serves 4

2 tablespoons ghee or argan oil
1 onion, finely chopped
¼ cup peeled, chopped ginger root
2–3 garlic cloves, finely chopped
2 teaspoons coriander seeds
1 teaspoon cumin seeds
1 teaspoon sugar
4 carrots, peeled and diced
¾ cup brown lentils, rinsed
1–2 teaspoons ras el hanout
1 (14½ oz) can diced tomatoes,
    drained of juice
5 cups hot chicken stock
bunch of cilantro, finely chopped
salt and black pepper

To serve

3–¼ cup plain yogurt
crusty bread

- Heat the ghee or oil in a heavy saucepan, stir in the onion, ginger, garlic, seeds, and sugar, and cook for 2–3 minutes. Add the carrots and cook for 2 minutes, stirring to coat well. Stir in the lentils, ras el hanout, tomatoes, and stock and bring to a boil, then reduce the heat and cook gently for 20 minutes.

- Season, stir in most of the chopped cilantro, and cook for another 5 minutes, until the carrots and lentils are tender. Swirl a little of the yogurt into the soup, then serve garnished with the remaining cilantro, with dollops of yogurt and crusty bread.

---

1 Lentils with Carrot and Cilantro Soup

Heat 1–2 tablespoons ghee in a saucepan, stir in 1 chopped onion, 2 chopped garlic cloves, 1 tablespoon chopped ginger root, 2 teaspoons dried red chile, 2 teaspoons coriander seeds, and 1 teaspoon sugar, and cook for 3–4 minutes. Add 2 cups cooked brown lentils and heat through. Season and stir in 2 tablespoons chopped cilantro. Meanwhile, heat through 6 cups prepared carrot and cilantro soup. Top with the lentils and dollops of plain yogurt.

2 Pureed Carrot and Cilantro Soup

Heat 2 tablespoons ghee or clarified butter in a heavy saucepan, stir in 1 finely chopped onion, 2 finely chopped garlic cloves, ¼ cup peeled and finely chopped fresh ginger root, 2 teaspoons coriander seeds, and 1 teaspoon sugar, and cook for 2–3 minutes. Add 16 peeled and diced carrots (about 2¼ lb), 1 teaspoon ras el hanout, a small bunch of cilantro leaves and stems, and 3½ cups hot chicken or vegetable stock, and bring to a boil, then cook over medium

heat for 15 minutes, until the carrots are tender. Puree the soup with an immersion blender or process in a blender. Return to the heat and season, then serve with dollops of plain yogurt, garnished with a little more finely chopped cilantro.

10 Chilled Almond and Garlic Soup

Serves 4

1 cup blanched almonds,
  coarsely chopped
3–4 slices of stale white bread,
  crusts removed
4 garlic cloves, coarsely chopped
¼ cup olive oil, plus extra to
  garnish
3½ cups chilled water or
  chicken stock
1–2 tablespoons white wine or
  apple vinegar
salt

To serve

ice cubes
seedless green grapes, sliced
1 red or green chile, seeded
  and finely sliced

- Put the blanched almonds into a food processor and process to a paste. Add the bread and garlic and replace the lid. With the motor running, drizzle in the oil through the feed tube, then gradually pour in the water or stock until the mixture has a smooth pouring consistency. Add the vinegar and season with salt.

- Put 2–3 ice cubes into each of 4 serving bowls, ladle the soup over them, and serve sprinkled with the grapes and chile and drizzled with olive oil.

20 Garlic, Almond, and Chorizo Soup

Heat 2 tablespoons olive oil in a saucepan, stir in 1 chopped onion, 3–4 chopped garlic cloves, 1 seeded and chopped red chile, and 2 teaspoons fennel seeds, and cook for 2–3 minutes. Add 12 oz sliced chorizo and cook for 1–2 minutes, then stir in 1 tablespoon tomato paste, 1–2 tablespoons ground almonds (almond meal), 3 cups hot chicken stock, and ²/₃ cup white wine and bring to a boil. Reduce the heat and simmer for 15 minutes. Season and serve garnished with cilantro.

30 Garlicky Chorizo and Potato Soup with Toasted Almonds

Dry-fry 2–3 tablespoons blanched almonds in a small, heavy skillet over medium heat for 3–4 minutes, until they turn golden brown and emit a nutty aroma. Using a mortar and pestle, coarsely grind the almonds. Set aside. Heat 2 tablespoons olive or argan oil in a heavy saucepan, stir in 1 finely chopped onion and 1 seeded and finely chopped red chile, and cook for 2–3 minutes. Add 8 oz thinly sliced chorizo and cook for 2 minutes, then stir in 4 crushed garlic cloves and 1–2 teaspoons smoked paprika. 1½ lb peeled and diced new potatoes and mix well, then pour in ²/₃ cup white wine and 3½ cups hot chicken stock. Bring to a boil, then cook over medium heat for 15–20 minutes, until the potatoes are tender. Season and stir in a finely chopped small bunch of flat leaf parsley. Sprinkle with the almonds and garnish with a little more finely chopped parsley.

MOR-SOUP-QAV

30 Apple and Butternut Soup with Chili Oil

Serves 4

3 green apples
1–2 tablespoons olive or argan oil
1½ tablespoons butter
1 onion, finely chopped
¼ cup peeled and finely chopped fresh ginger root
2 teaspoons fennel seeds
1 teaspoon coriander seeds
1 teaspoon cumin seeds
1 teaspoon sugar
1 small butternut squash, peeled, seeded, and diced
4 cups hot chicken stock
⅔ cup heavy cream
salt and black pepper
chili oil, for drizzling

- Core and finely slice 1 of the apples horizontally to form thin disks. Place on a wire rack set over a baking sheet and bake in a preheated oven, at 300°F, for 20–25 minutes. Peel, core, and dice the remaining apples.

- Meanwhile, heat the oil and butter in a heavy saucepan, stir in the onion, ginger, seeds, and sugar, and cook for 1–2 minutes. Add the squash and cook for 2–3 minutes, stirring to coat well. Add the diced apples and stock and bring to a boil, then cook over medium heat for 20 minutes.

- Stir in the cream and season. Ladle into 4 serving bowls, add baked apple slices to each, and drizzle with a little chili oil.

---

10 Applesauce with Chili Oil

Put 1¼ cups store-bought, chilled applesauce, the juice of 1 lemon, 2 tablespoons orange blossom water, and a finely chopped small bunch each of mint and cilantro in a bowl. Season with a little salt and black pepper and add a little sugar or honey, if necessary. Spoon the mixture into a bowl and serve with a drizzle of chili oil as an appetizer or a sauce for broiled or roasted meat.

20 Pureed Apple Soup with Chili Oil

Heat 2 tablespoons olive oil and a pat of butter in a heavy saucepan, stir in 1 finely chopped onion, 2 finely chopped garlic cloves, 2 teaspoons fennel seeds, and 1–2 teaspoons sugar, and cook for 2–3 minutes. Add 5–6 peeled, cored, and diced Pippin, McIntosh, or Fuji apples and 3½ cups hot chicken or vegetable stock and bring to a boil, then cook over medium heat for 12–15 minutes, until the apple is soft. Puree the soup with an immersion blender or process in a blender. Return to the heat, season, and add a little more sugar if the apples are tart. Drizzle with a little chili oil and serve as an appetizer or between courses.

MOR-SOUP-SAY

30 Chile and Fino Gazpacho

Serves 4

6 tomatoes

1 small cucumber, peeled,
   seeded, and diced

1 red bell pepper, seeded
   and diced

1 onion, finely chopped

2 red or green chiles, seeded
   and finely chopped

2 garlic cloves, crushed

2 tablespoons olive oil

juice of 1 lemon

1 teaspoon Tabasco sauce

3 cups chilled tomato juice

¼ cup fino sherry

1–2 teaspoons sugar

salt and black pepper

To serve

ice cubes (optional)

3–4 tablespoons plain yogurt

small bunch of cilantro,
   finely chopped

- Put the tomatoes into a heatproof bowl and pour enough boiling water over them to cover. Let stand for 1–2 minutes, then drain, cut a cross at the stem end of each tomato, and peel off the skins. Cut into quarters, remove the seeds, and finely dice the flesh.

- Put the tomatoes into a bowl with the cucumber, red bell pepper, onion, chiles, and garlic. Add the oil, lemon juice, and Tabasco and mix well. Put one-third of the mixture into a food processor with half the tomato juice and process to a puree. Return to the bowl and combine with the remaining tomato juice and the sherry. Season with salt and black pepper and add sugar to taste. Cover and chill for at least 15 minutes.

- Spoon the gazpacho into 4 serving bowls, adding an ice cube to each if not sufficiently chilled. Serve with dollops of yogurt and sprinkled with the cilantro.

---

1 **Gazpacho with Herb and Chile Relish** Finely chop a large bunch of cilantro and a small bunch of mint and place in a bowl. Add 2 finely chopped and seeded green chiles and 1 teaspoon sea salt and mix well. Stir half the relish into 2½ cups store-bought chilled gazpacho. Put some crushed ice into 2 glasses, pour the soup over them, and sprinkle with the remaining relish.

2 **Quick Chile and Fino Gazpacho** Peel, seed, and coarsely chop 1 small cucumber and put into a food processor. Coarsely chop 1 onion, 1 seeded red or green bell pepper, 2 seeded red or green chiles, and 2 garlic cloves and add to the processor with 1 tablespoon tomato paste, 1–2 teaspoons sugar, 2 tablespoons olive oil, and the juice of 1 lemon. Process to a thick puree, then gradually pour in 2½ cups chilled tomato juice and ¼ cup fino sherry and season to taste. Cover and chill for at least 10 minutes, or serve with ice cubes. Garnish with a small bunch of cilantro, finely chopped, and serve with a glass of fino sherry.

30 Chicken, Nut, and Cinnamon Pie

Serves 4

2–3 tablespoons olive oil

1 stick butter

3 onions, finely sliced

2 garlic cloves, finely chopped

2 teaspoons coriander seeds

2–3 tablespoons blanched
   almonds, chopped

3 teaspoons ground cinnamon

1 teaspoon ground ginger

1 teaspoon paprika

10 oz skinless, boneless chicken
   breasts, cut into chunks

1–2 tablespoons orange
   blossom water

small bunch of flat leaf parsley,
   finely chopped

bunch of cilantro, finely chopped

7–8 sheets of phyllo pastry

1 egg yolk mixed with a little water

salt and black pepper

2 teaspoons confectioners' sugar,
   for dusting

- Heat the oil and a pat of the butter in a heavy skillet, stir in the onions, garlic, and coriander seeds, and cook for 2–3 minutes. Stir in the almonds, 2 teaspoons ground cinnamon, the ground ginger, and paprika, then add the chicken and coat well. Add the orange blossom water, reduce the heat and cook gently for 3–4 minutes, until almost dry. Toss in the herbs and season.

- Melt the remaining butter in a small saucepan. Separate the sheets of phyllo and place under a clean, damp dish towel to prevent them from drying out. Brush a little butter over the bottom of a round ovenproof dish and cover with 1 sheet of phyllo, flopping the sides over the edge. Brush with butter and place another sheet on top. Repeat with another 2 layers. Spread the chicken mixture over the pastry, then fold over the edges. Cover with the remaining phyllo, brushing with butter. Tuck the overlapping edges under the pie, then brush with the egg wash.

- Bake in a preheated oven, at 400°F, for about 20 minutes, until the pastry is puffed and golden. Dust with the remaining ground cinnamon, followed by the sugar.

---

10 **Simple Chicken, Nut, and Cinnamon Wraps** Place 4 tortilla wraps on a flat surface and fill with 1²/₃ cups cooked thin chicken strips, sliced onion, a sprinkling of chopped mixed nuts, coarsely chopped flat leaf parsley and cilantro, dollops of thick plain yogurt, and a little harissa paste. Roll up and dust with cinnamon to serve.

---

20 **Warm Chicken, Nut, and Cinnamon Wraps** Heat 2 tablespoons oil in a heavy skillet, stir in 1 finely chopped onion, 2 finely chopped garlic cloves, 1 tablespoon peeled and finely chopped fresh ginger root, and 2 teaspoons coriander seeds, and cook for 2–3 minutes. Add 10 oz finely sliced skinless, boneless chicken breasts and cook for 2–3 minutes, then stir in 1–2 teaspoons ground cinnamon, 1 teaspoon paprika, and 2 tablespoons mixed chopped nuts. Season, cover, and cook gently for 3–4 minutes. Place 4 warmed tortilla wraps on a flat surface, drizzle with a little chili oil or smear with a little harissa paste (see page 70), then sprinkle with chopped cilantro. Spoon the chicken mixture over the wraps, then roll up. Serve with spicy dips, pickles, or chutneys.

Feta, Olive, and Preserved Lemon Pastries

Serves 4

1 sheet chilled ready-to-bake
   puff pastry
flour, for dusting
olive oil, for brushing
1 cup crumbled feta cheese
2 tablespoons finely chopped,
   pitted black ripe olives
finely chopped rind of 1 preserved
   lemon (see page 68)
2 teaspoons dried mint

- Roll out the pastry on a lightly floured surface to a rectangle about ¼ inch thick, then cut into 8 thin strips. Place them on lightly oiled baking sheets and brush each strip with a little oil.

- In a small bowl, gently mix together the feta, olives, preserved lemon rind, and half the mint. Sprinkle a thin layer of the mixture over each pastry strip, then put into a preheated oven, at 400°F, for 12–15 minutes, until the pastry is cooked. Sprinkle the remaining mint over the tops and serve hot.

 Feta, Olive, and Preserved Lemon Toasted Pitas Lightly toast 4 pita breads or other flatbreads. Melt 1–2 tablespoons butter or ghee in a small saucepan and brush a little over each bread. Sprinkle 1 cup crumbled feta cheese, 2 tablespoons chopped, pitted black ripe olives, and the finely chopped rind of 1 preserved lemon (see page 68) over the bread and serve sprinkled with mint and flat leaf parsley leaves.

 Feta, Olive, and Preserved Lemon Pastry Roll Roll out 1 sheet chilled ready-to-bake puff pastry on a lightly floured surface to a rectangle about ⅛ inch thick. In a bowl, mix together 1 cup crumbled feta cheese, 2 tablespoons finely chopped, pitted black ripe olives, the finely chopped rind of 1 preserved lemon (see page 68), and a finely chopped small bunch each of mint and flat leaf parsley, then add 1 egg and mix well. Spoon the mixture along a long edge of the pastry. Roll the edge over the mixture, fold over the short edges, and roll up the pastry so that it resembles a long, stuffed log. Place on a lightly oiled baking sheet and brush with a little olive oil. Using a sharp knife, carefully make several short slashes on the top of the pastry. Place in a preheated oven, at 400°F, for 20–25 minutes, until cooked and browned.

Deep-Fried Fish and Chermoula Pastries

Serves 4

1 lb skinless cod or halibut
  fillets, boned and cut into
  bite-size pieces
1 sheet phyllo pastry, cut into
  4 inch squares
4 tablespoons butter, melted
sunflower oil, for deep-frying
salt and black pepper
chili dipping sauce, to serve

For the chermoula

2 tablespoons olive oil
juice of 1 lemon
1 teaspoon ground cumin
1 teaspoon smoked paprika
1 red chile, seeded and chopped
finely chopped rind of ½ preserved
  lemon (see page 68)
2 garlic cloves, crushed
1 tablespoon chopped cilantro
1 tablespoon chopped parsley

- Mix together all the chermoula ingredients in a bowl. Toss in the fish pieces and season well.

- Lay out the phyllo under a clean, damp dish towel to prevent the pastry from drying out. Place 1 phyllo square on a flat surface and brush it with a little melted butter, then put another on top at an angle and brush it with more butter. Repeat with a third sheet at an angle. Place a small spoonful of the fish in the center and carefully pull up the edges, pinching the ends together using wet fingertips. Repeat with the remaining ingredients to make 16–20 pastries.

- In a large, deep saucepan, heat enough oil for deep-frying to 350–375°F or until a cube of bread browns in 30 seconds. Deep-fry the pastries in batches for 2–3 minutes, until lightly browned. Remove with a slotted spoon and drain on paper towels. Serve hot with a drizzle of chili oil, a little harissa paste, or a dipping sauce.

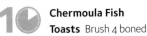 **Chermoula Fish Toasts** Brush 4 boned skinless cod or halibut fillets with olive oil and season. Cook under a preheated medium broiler for 2–3 minutes on each side, until cooked through. Meanwhile, toast 4 flatbreads and drizzle with olive oil. Place the fish on the toasts and drizzle with 1 tablespoon prepared chermoula paste. Sprinkle with the chopped rind of ½ preserved lemon (see page 68) and serve.

 Baked Fish and Chermoula Pastries Toss 1 lb skinless cod or halibut fillets, boned and cut into bite-size chunks, in 2 tablespoons prepared chermoula paste and season well. Lay out 8 sheets of phyllo pastry under a clean, damp dish towel to prevent them from drying out. Place 1 sheet on a flat surface and brush the top with a little olive or sunflower oil, then put ⅛ of the fish mixture in the center. Fold over 2 sides to enclose the filling, then pull over the other sides to form a square package. Brush the edges with a little water and stick together. Repeat with the remaining ingredients. Place the packages, seam side down, in a lightly oiled baking dish. Brush with a little more oil and place in a preheated oven, at 400°F, for 20 minutes, until crisp and golden brown.

MOR-SOUP-TYC

 Mini Lamb and Harissa Pizzas

Serves 4

6 oz lean ground lamb
1 onion, finely chopped
2 garlic cloves, crushed
2 teaspoons cumin seeds
1 teaspoon ground coriander
1 teaspoon ground fenugreek
1–2 teaspoons harissa paste
  (see page 70)
1 tablespoon olive oil, plus
  extra for greasing
4 store-bought individual
  pizza crusts
2 teaspoons tomato paste
small bunch of cilantro,
  finely chopped
salt and black pepper

- Mix together the lamb, onion, garlic, spices, and harissa in a bowl. Add the oil, mix well, and season, then knead to a sticky paste.

- Put the pizza crusts onto a lightly oiled baking sheet and lightly smear with the tomato paste, then spread a thin layer of the meat mixture over each.

- Put into a preheated oven, at 425°F, for 12–15 minutes. Sprinkle the chopped cilantro over the tops and serve hot.

Lamb and Harissa Toasts

Heat 2 tablespoons olive oil in a skillet, stir in 1 chopped onion, 2 chopped garlic cloves, 1 teaspoon each of cumin seeds and sugar, and cook for 2 minutes. Stir in 1–2 teaspoons harissa paste (see page 70) and 8 oz ground lamb and cook, stirring, for 5–6 minutes. Season and toss in a finely chopped small bunch of cilantro. Meanwhile, toast 4 slices of crusty bread and drizzle with a little olive oil. Spoon the lamb over the toast, garnish with a little more cilantro, and serve with dollops of plain yogurt, pickles, or chutney.

Lamb and Harissa Rolls

Using a large mortar and pestle, pound 12 oz lean ground lamb with 2 crushed garlic cloves, 2 teaspoons ground cumin, 1 teaspoon ground coriander, 1 teaspoon ground fenugreek, and 2 teaspoons harissa paste (see page 70). Alternatively, process together in a food processor. Mix in a finely chopped small bunch of flat leaf parsley and 1 tablespoon olive oil to make a smooth paste, then season. Roll out 1 sheet of chilled ready-to-back puff pastry on a lightly floured surface to about 15 x 10 inches. Spread the meat paste in a thin layer over the pastry, taking it right to the edges. Starting from a long edge, roll up the pastry into a log. Using a sharp knife, slice into bite-size portions and place on a lightly oiled baking sheet. Bake in a preheated oven, at 400°F, for 15–20 minutes, until puffed and golden brown. Serve hot with chili dipping sauce and chutneys.

MOR-SOUP-XUT

 Chorizo and Parsley Eggs

Serves 4

1 tablespoon ghee or butter
1 lb chorizo or merguez sausage,
  thinly sliced diagonally
8 eggs
large bunch of flat leaf parsley,
  coarsely chopped
salt and black pepper

- Heat the ghee or butter in a large, heavy skillet, stir in the sausage, and cook for 2–3 minutes.

- Break the eggs into the skillet, cover, and cook over medium heat for 4–5 minutes, until the whites are firm. Season, sprinkle with the parsley and serve hot.

 Quick Potato and Parsley Omelet

Put 1 (14½ oz) can new potatoes into a bowl and mash to a coarse paste. In a bowl, beat together 8 eggs and ⅔ cup milk, then stir in 1 tablespoon finely chopped flat leaf parsley and 1 teaspoon smoked paprika. Season well and beat into the mashed potatoes. Heat 1–2 tablespoons ghee or butter in a flameproof, heavy skillet, add the potato mixture, cover, and cook gently for 8–10 minutes, until firm. Remove the lid, dot with a little butter, and put under a preheated medium broiler for 3–4 minutes, until browned. Divide into 4 and garnish with a little more chopped parsley.

 Potato, Chorizo, and Parsley

Omelet Cook 4–5 new potatoes in a saucepan of boiling water for 8–10 minutes, or until tender. Drain, refresh under cold running water, and drain again, then peel off the skins and cut into thin slices. In a bowl, beat together 8 eggs and 1¼ cups milk, then stir in 2 tablespoons finely chopped flat leaf parsley and season. Heat 1–2 tablespoons ghee or butter in a heavy skillet, stir in 1 teaspoon cumin seeds and 1 teaspoon fennel seeds and cook for 1–2 minutes. Add 8 oz thinly sliced chorizo and cook for 1–2 minutes, then add the potatoes, coat well, and cook for another 1–2 minutes. Pour in the egg mixture, cover, and cook over low heat for 10–12 minutes, moving the mixture occasionally, until firm. Turn off the heat and let stand, still covered, for a few minutes. Divide into 4 and garnish with a little more finely chopped parsley or cilantro.

MOR-SOUP-HEH

30 Zucchini, Mint, and Bread Omelet

Serves 4–6

2 zucchini, thinly sliced

2 tablespoons olive oil

4 tablespoons butter

1 onion, sliced

small bunch of mint,
  coarsely chopped

6 eggs

2 slices of white bread, crusts
  removed, soaked in a little milk

salt and black pepper

1 scant teaspoon paprika,
  for dusting

- Place the zucchini in a colander and sprinkle with a little salt to draw out the juices. Let stand for about 5 minutes, then rinse and pat dry.

- Heat the oil and a little of the butter in a heavy skillet, stir in the onion, and cook for 2–3 minutes, until softened. Add the zucchini and cook for another 3–4 minutes, until golden brown. Toss in the mint and let cool slightly.

- Beat the eggs lightly in a bowl. Squeeze the bread dry and add to the eggs, crumbling it with your fingers. Beat well, season and stir in the cooled zucchini mixture.

- Melt the remaining butter in the skillet, add the egg mixture, cover, and cook gently for 10–15 minutes, until set. Dust with the paprika, then cut diagonally into diamond shapes and serve.

10 Herbed Zucchini Eggs

Heat 2 tablespoons olive oil and a pat of butter in a heavy skillet, stir in 1 sliced zucchini ,and cook for 3–4 minutes, until it begins to brown. Toss in a finely chopped small bunch each of mint, dill, and flat leaf parsley, then make 4 wells in the mixture. Break 4 eggs into the wells, cover, and cook for 4–5 minutes, until the whites are firm. Season to taste, garnish with a little more finely chopped mint and dill, and serve immediately.

20 Herb and Bread Omelet

Soak 2 slices of white bread in a little milk for 2–3 minutes. Lightly beat 6 eggs in a bowl. Squeeze the bread dry and crumble it with your fingers into the eggs. Add a coarsely chopped small bunch each of flat leaf parsley and mint and several coarsely chopped dill sprigs. Season well and mix thoroughly. Heat 2 tablespoons olive oil in a heavy skillet, add the egg mixture, cover, and cook gently for 10–15 minutes, until set. Dust with a little paprika, then cut into 4 and serve.

MOR-SOUP-GUL

Chile and Herb Sweet Potato Pancakes

Serves 4

1¼ cups all-purpose flour
3 eggs, lightly beaten
½ cup milk
1 tablespoon olive oil
2 sweet potatoes, peeled and
  coarsely grated
2 onions, finely sliced
1 red or green chile, seeded and
  finely sliced
4–6 sage leaves, finely chopped
1 tablespoon thyme leaves
sunflower oil, for frying
salt and black pepper
sumac, for sprinkling (optional)

• Sift the flour into a bowl, make a well in the center, and pour in the eggs. Gradually add the milk, beating continuously to form a smooth batter. Beat in the olive oil. Add the sweet potatoes, onions, chile, sage, and thyme, season well with salt and black pepper, and mix thoroughly.

• Heat a little sunflower oil in a skillet, swirling it evenly over the bottom. When hot, pour in 3–4 small ladlefuls of the batter and press each flat. Cook for 2–3 minutes on each side, until golden brown, then drain on paper towels. Repeat with the remaining batter to make 6–8 pancakes. Serve sprinkled with sea salt or sumac.

 Sweet Potato Chips with Chile and Herb Honey Peel and finely slice 1 sweet potato into disks. In a deep saucepan, heat enough sunflower oil for deep-frying to 350–375°F or until a cube of bread browns in 30 seconds. Deep-fry the sweet potatoes in batches for 2–3 minutes, until lightly brown. Meanwhile, heat together 2–3 tablespoons honey, 1 tablespoon finely crumbled dried sage, and 1 teaspoon finely chopped dried red chile in a small saucepan. Remove the chips with a slotted spoon and drain on paper towels. Transfer to a plate, drizzle with the sage honey, and serve.

 Sweet Potato, Chile, and Herb Pancakes Sift ¼ cup all-purpose flour and a pinch of salt into a bowl, make a well in the center, and pour in 1 lightly beaten egg. Gradually beat in ⅔ cup milk to form a smooth batter. Add a few drops of olive oil, 1 peeled and coarsely grated sweet potato, 1–2 teaspoons finely chopped dried red chile, and 1 tablespoon each of dried thyme and finely crumbled dried sage and mix well. Cover and let stand for 10 minutes. Heat a nonstick skillet, wipe it with a little sunflower oil, and add a ladleful of the batter, swirling it around to form a thin layer.

Cook for 1–2 minutes on each side, until golden brown. Transfer to a plate and keep warm. Repeat with the remaining batter to make about 4 pancakes, adding a little more oil, if necessary. Meanwhile, heat 2–3 tablespoons honey in a small saucepan. Roll up the pancakes, drizzle a little honey over them, and serve.

Soft-Boiled Eggs with Harissa

Serves 4

4 eggs
4 slices of bread
4 heaping teaspoons harissa paste
(see page 70)

- Place the eggs in a saucepan of water, bring to a boil, and cook for 3–5 minutes, depending on how you prefer your eggs. Meanwhile, toast the bread and cut into long strips.

- Drain the eggs, cut them in half, and serve on a plate with the strips of toast and a small bowl of harissa. To eat, first dip the strips of toast into the harissa, then dip into the egg.

 Spiced Fried Eggs with Harissa Toast

Dry-fry 2 teaspoons cumin seeds in a small, heavy skillet over medium heat for 2 minutes, until they emit a nutty aroma. Break 8 eggs into a bowl without beating. Heat 1–2 tablespoons ghee or smen in a heavy skillet, stir in 2–3 crushed garlic cloves, and cook for 1–2 minutes, until it begins to brown. Stir in the toasted seeds for 1 minute, then slide in the eggs. Sprinkle 1 teaspoon each of sea salt and dried mint over the eggs, cover, and cook over low heat for 5 minutes, or until set. Toast 4 flatbreads or 4 slices of bread, then spread a thin layer of harissa paste (see page 70) over each. Divide the eggs into 4 and place onto the toast. Serve immediately with a little more harissa, if desired.

 Spiced Hard-Boiled Eggs with Harissa Bring a saucepan of water to a boil, carefully lower in 4–8 eggs, and bring back to a boil, then cook for 8–10 minutes. Meanwhile, dry-fry 2 teaspoons cumin seeds and 1 teaspoon coriander seeds in a small, heavy skillet over medium heat for 2 minutes, until they emit a nutty aroma. Using a mortar and pestle or spice grinder, coarsely grind the spices. Drain the eggs and refresh under cold running water, then shell. Heat 1–2 tablespoons ghee, smen, clarified butter, or argan oil in a heavy skillet, stir in 2 crushed garlic cloves, and cook for 1–2 minutes. Add the crushed spices and cook for 1 minute, then add the eggs, rolling them in the garlic and spices. Cover and cook over low heat for 10 minutes, rolling the eggs occasionally. Dust the eggs with a little cinnamon and serve with a small bowl of harissa paste (see page 70) for dipping.

 Chile, Lime, and Cilantro
Dried Fruit and Nuts

Serves 4

1 cup whole almonds

2 tablespoons ghee, clarified butter, or smen

2 tablespoons macadamia nuts, halved

2 tablespoons cashew nuts, halved

1 cup dried apricots

1 cup pitted dates

1–2 teaspoons finely chopped dried red chile

grated rind of 1 lime

small bunch of cilantro, finely chopped

salt

- Put the almonds into a bowl and pour enough boiling water over them to cover. Let stand for 5 minutes, then drain, refresh under cold running water, and drain again. Using your fingers, rub the skins off the almonds and cut in half.

- Heat the ghee, butter, or smen in a large, heavy skillet, add the nuts and dried fruit, and cook, stirring, for 4–5 minutes, until the nuts begin to brown. Toss in the chile and lime rind and cook for another 2–3 minutes, then season with salt and add the cilantro. Serve immediately.

 Chili Oil and Cilantro Mixed Nuts Heat 2 tablespoons chili oil in a heavy saucepan. Add 2–3 cups mixed nuts, such as almonds, cashews, macadamia, and hazelnuts, and cook until they begin to brwon. Season with salt to taste and toss in 1 tablespoon finely chopped cilantro. Transfer to a bowl and serve.

 Nut-Stuffed Dates with Chili Oil and Cilantro Put 2 cups ground almonds or pistachio nuts, 1 cup sifted confectioners' sugar, 1 teaspoon ground cumin, 1 beaten egg, and 1–2 teaspoons lemon juice in a bowl. Using your fingers, mix together to form a sticky paste, then transfer to a surface lightly dusted with confectioners' sugar and knead until smooth. Shape small pieces of the paste into oblongs, then stuff into 12–16 pitted dates. Heat 2 tablespoons chili oil in a heavy skillet, add the dates, stuffed side up, cover, and cook over medium heat for 4–5 minutes, until heated through. Season with salt and stir in a finely chopped small bunch of cilantro.

3 Parsnip and Beet Chips with Homemade Dukkah

Serves 4

sunflower or vegetable oil,
for deep-frying

2 parsnips, peeled, halved, and
thinly sliced lengthwise

2–3 raw beets, peeled and
thinly sliced

salt and black pepper

For the spice mix

1 tablespoon hazelnuts

1 tablespoon sesame seeds

2 teaspoons cumin seeds

2 teaspoons coriander seeds

2 teaspoons dried mint

- To make the spice mix, dry-fry the hazelnuts and seeds in a small, heavy skillet over medium heat for 2–3 minutes, until they emit a nutty aroma. Using a mortar and pestle, pound the nuts and seeds to a coarse powder, or put into a spice grinder and grind to a fine powder. Stir in the mint and season well. Set aside.

- In a deep saucepan, heat enough oil for deep-frying to 350–375°F or until a cube of bread browns in 30 seconds. Deep-fry the parsnips in batches until lightly browned. Remove with a slotted spoon and drain on paper towels, then transfer all the parsnips into a bowl while hot and sprinkle half the dukkah spice mix over the chips.

- Reduce the heat (the beet slices burn easily) and deep-fry the beets in batches. Remove and drain as above, then transfer to a bowl and sprinkle with the remaining spice mix. Serve the parsnip and beet chips separately or mixed together.

1 Fried Bread and Dukkah Bites

Remove the crusts of 4–8 slices of stale bread and cut them into bite-size squares. Heat enough oil for deep-frying as above. Deep-fry the bread in batches until golden brown. Remove with a slotted spoon and drain on paper towels, then transfer to a bowl while hot and toss with 1–2 tablespoons prepared dukkah spice mix (for homemade, see above). Add salt or dried mint to taste and serve.

2 Baked Cheese and Dukkah Puffs

Put 1¼ sticks butter, 1¾ cups shredded cheddar cheese (or a firm sheep cheese), 1¾ cups all-purpose flour, 1 egg yolk, and 1 teaspoon ground cumin in a food processor and season. Pulse together until the mixture resembles coarse bread crumbs. Roll a little of the mixture into a small ball, then flatten in the palm of your hand. Place on a baking sheet lined with parchment paper (you may need 2 sheets). Repeat with the remaining mixture to make about 20–30 disks. Put into a preheated oven, at 350°F, for 10 minutes, until lightly browned and slightly puffed. Meanwhile, mix together 1 tablespoon dukkah spice mix (for homemade, see above), 1 teaspoon paprika, and 1 teaspoon dried mint (if not already in the mix), then sprinkle over the cheese puffs. Let cool until firm on the sheets before serving.

1 Popcorn with Chili Oil

Serves 4

1–2 tablespoons chili oil,
  plus extra for drizzling
1²⁄₃ cups popping corn
1 teaspoon sea salt

- Pour a thin layer of chili oil into a heavy saucepan. Add enough corn to form a single layer in the pan—the quantity of oil and corn will vary according to the size of your pan. Cover with a lid and place over medium heat, shaking the pan occasionally as the corn pops.

- When the popping stops, remove the lid and toss in a little salt to taste. Transfer the popcorn to a bowl, finish with an extra drizzle of chili oil, and serve.

 2 Popcorn with Chile Honey

Put 3–4 tablespoons honey and 2 teaspoons finely chopped dried red chile or 2–3 whole dried red chiles in a small saucepan and heat until the honey begins to bubble. Turn off the heat and let stand for 10 minutes to let the flavors mingle. Pour a thin layer of sunflower or vegetable oil into a large, heavy saucepan. Add enough popping corn to form a single layer in the pan. Cover with a lid and place over medium heat, shaking the pan occasionally as the corn pops. When the popping stops, remove the lid and season with salt to taste, then transfer to a bowl. Reheat the honey, pour over the popcorn, and serve.

 3 Corn Cobs with Chile and Thyme

Butter Peel off the husks from 4 fresh ears of corn, then pull off the silks and cut off the stems. Cook in a saucepan of unsalted boiling water for 5 minutes. Meanwhile, beat together 2 tablespoons softened butter or smen, the juice of ½ lemon, 1–2 teaspoons finely chopped dried red chile, 2 teaspoons dried thyme, and 1–2 crushed garlic cloves in a bowl, then season well. Drain the corn, then refresh under cold running water and pat dry. Smear the chile and thyme butter over the corn, then put into a baking pan. Place in a preheated oven, at 350°F, for 15 minutes, turning occasionally until golden brown. Serve hot.

Cheese and Paprika Potato Cakes

Serves 4

12 small russet or Yukon
  gold potatoes
8 oz hard, tangy sheep or sharp
  cheddar cheese, finely diced
1–2 teaspoon cumin seeds
2 teaspoons smoked paprika
¼ cup all-purpose flour
sunflower or vegetable oil,
  for pan-frying
salt and black pepper
lemon wedges, to garnish
dips or condiments, to serve
  (optional)

- Cook the potatoes in a saucepan of boiling water for 10–12 minutes, until soft. Drain, then refresh under cold running water and peel off the skins. Put into a bowl and coarsely mash with a fork until still a little chunky. Add the cheese, cumin seeds, and paprika and season.

- Place the flour on a plate. Divide the potato mixture into 12 pieces, shape each piece into a ball, then flatten slightly and dip into the flour to lightly coat on both sides.

- Heat a thin layer of oil in a large, heavy skillet, add the potato cakes, and cook for about 8 minutes, turning occasionally, until crispy and golden brown. Drain on paper towels, sprinkle with a little extra sea salt, garnish with lemon wedges, and serve with dips or condiments, if desired.

 **Paprika and Herb Cheese**
Put 10 oz feta cheese, cut into bite-size pieces, into a shallow serving dish. Drizzle with 2 tablespoons olive oil, dust with 1–2 teaspoons hot paprika, and sprinkle a finely chopped small bunch of flat leaf parsley over the top. Serve with chunks of crusty bread to mop up the oil.

 Paprika and Herb Cheesy Mashed Potatoes Cook 6 russet or Yukon gold potatoes, peeled and coarsely chopped, in a saucepan of boiling water for about 10 minutes, until soft. Drain, then return to the pan and coarsely mash with a fork. Beat in 1¾ cups shredded hard sheep or cheddar cheese or crumbled feta cheese while the potatoes are still hot. Add 1–2 teaspoons smoked paprika and a finely chopped small bunch of flat leaf parsley and season. Serve with dollops of creamy yogurt and pickled chiles.

QuickCook

Couscous, K'dras, and Tagines

Recipes listed by cooking time

10

10 Quick Cinnamon Couscous

Serves 4

2 cups couscous
2 tablespoons butter or ghee
1 teaspoon cinnamon
1 teaspoon confectioners' sugar
(optional)
salt and black pepper

- Put the couscous into a heatproof bowl and just cover with boiling water. Cover with plastic wrap and let stand for 5 minutes, then fluff up with a fork.

- Melt the butter or ghee in a large skillet, add the couscous, stirring well to separate the grains, and season.

- Spoon the couscous into a pyramid on a serving dish and dust with the cinnamon and confectioners' sugar, if using. Serve hot as a side dish.

 2 Buttered Almond and Cinnamon Couscous Put 2 cups couscous into a bowl. Stir ½ teaspoon salt into 1¾ cups warm water, pour it over the couscous, and mix well. Cover with a clean dish towel and let stand for about 10 minutes. Melt 2 tablespoons butter or ghee in a heavy skillet, stir in 2 tablespoons slivered almonds, and cook for 2–3 minutes, until golden brown. Add the couscous and toss well. Serve hot as a side dish, dusted with a little ground cinnamon.

 3 Buttery Couscous with Cinnamon Put 2 cups couscous into an ovenproof dish. Stir ½ teaspoon salt into 1¾ cups warm water and pour it over the couscous. Cover with a clean dish towel and let stand for about 10 minutes. Using your fingers, rub 2 tablespoons sunflower or olive oil into the grains to break up the lumps. Lift the couscous into the air and let it fall back into the dish so that the grains feel light and airy. Sprinkle 2 tablespoons butter, cut into small pieces, over the grains and cover with a piece of damp parchment paper. Put into a preheated oven, at 350°F, for about 15 minutes, until heated through. Fluff up with a fork and serve as a side dish, dusted with 1 scant teaspoon cinnamon.

Spicy Pine Nut and Apricot Couscous

Serves 4

1–2 tablespoons butter or ghee

1 teaspoon cumin seeds

1 teaspoon coriander seeds

1 teaspoon fennel seeds

2 tablespoons toasted pine nuts

2–3 tablespoons finely chopped dried apricots

1–2 teaspoons harissa paste (see page 70)

salt and black pepper

For the couscous

2 cups couscous

½ teaspoon salt

1¾ cups warm water

1–2 tablespoons sunflower oil

- Put the couscous into a heatproof bowl. Stir the salt into the measured water and pour it over the couscous. Cover with a clean dish towel and let stand for about 10 minutes. Using your fingers, rub the oil into the grains for 4–5 minutes, until light, airy, and any lumps are broken up.

- Heat the butter or ghee in a heavy skillet, stir in the spices, and sauté for 2 minutes, until they emit a nutty aroma. Toss in the pine nuts, apricots, and harissa, then add the couscous, mix well, and season.

Quick Spicy Pine Nut Couscous

Put 2 cups couscous into a heatproof bowl and just cover with boiling water. Cover with plastic wrap and let stand for 5 minutes, then fluff up with a fork. Heat 1–2 tablespoons ghee in a large, heavy skillet, add 2 teaspoons harissa paste (see page 70), stir in the couscous, mix well, and cook until heated through. Season, then serve sprinkled with 1 tablespoon toasted pine nuts.

Spicy Pistachio, Pine Nut, and Date Couscous Prepare 2 cups couscous as above. Dry-fry 1 cup shelled, unsalted pistachio nuts and 2 tablespoons pine nuts in a heavy skillet over medium heat until they begin to brown and emit a nutty aroma. Melt 1–2 tablespoons ghee or butter in a separate large, heavy saucepan, stir in the toasted pistachios, most of the pine nuts, and 1 teaspoon cardamom seeds. Stir in ¾ cup finely sliced, pitted dates, a pinch of saffron threads, and 1–2 teaspoons ras el hanout and cook for 1–2 minutes. Add the prepared couscous, mix well, and heat through, then season. Turn off the heat, cover with a clean dish towel, and let steam for 5 minutes. Toss over high heat, then serve sprinkled with the reserved pine nuts and sprinkled with 2 teaspoons ground cinnamon. Serve immediately.

3⏺ Couscous Tfaia with Beef

Serves 4

1 lb beef, cut into strips
1 onion, finely chopped
1 teaspoon ground coriander
1 teaspoon ground cumin
pinch of saffron threads
1 quantity couscous (see
    30-minute recipe, page 134)

For the tfaia

1 teaspoon saffron threads
2 tablespoons warm water
1 tablespoon olive oil
1 tablespoon butter
2 onions, thinly sliced
2 tablespoons golden raisins
2–3 cinnamon sticks
2 tablespoons honey
salt and black pepper

- Place the beef in a heavy saucepan or the bottom of a tagine with the onion and spices. Pour in just enough water to cover and bring to a boil. Reduce the heat, cover, and simmer for 25–30 minutes.

- Meanwhile, prepare and cook the couscous following the 30-minute method on page 134.

- To make the tfaia, put the saffron in a small bowl, add the measured water, and let soak. Heat the oil and butter in a heavy skillet, stir in the onions, and cook for 2–3 minutes. Add the golden raisins, cinnamon sticks, saffron water, and honey and season. Reduce the heat, cover, and cook gently for 10–15 minutes.

- Remove the beef from the cooking liquid, spoon the meat over the couscous on a serving plate, and top with the tfaia. Strain the liquid into a small bowl and serve separately.

1⏺ Simple Harissa Beef Couscous

Heat 2 tablespoons ghee in a heavy skillet, stir in 2 finely chopped garlic cloves and 1 tablespoon peeled and finely chopped fresh ginger root, and cook for 2–3 minutes. Stir in 8 oz lean beef, finely sliced, and cook for 2–3 minutes. Meanwhile, put 2 cups couscous into a heatproof bowl and just cover with boiling water. Cover with plastic wrap and let stand for 5 minutes, then fluff up with a fork. Add the couscous with 1–2 teaspoons harissa paste (see page 70) to the beef, mix well, and heat through. Season and serve garnished with some finely chopped cilantro.

2⏺ Couscous Tfaia

Heat 2 tablespoons ghee in a skillet, stir in 3 sliced onions and 1 tablespoon chopped fresh ginger root, and cook for 3–4 minutes. Add 2 tablespoons golden raisins, 3–4 cinnamon sticks, 1 teaspoon saffron threads soaked in 2 tablespoons water, and 2 tablespoons honey. Cover and cook gently for 10–15 minutes. Season. Meanwhile, prepare 2 cups couscous following the 20-minute method on page 138, omitting the lemon rind and black pepper. Serve with the tfaia, garnished with chopped cilantro.

MOR-COUS-XYM

30 Couscous with Spring Vegetables and Dill

Serves 4

3½ cups hot vegetable or
    chicken stock
pinch of saffron threads
1 cup shelled fresh fava beans
2–3 fresh or frozen prepared
    artichoke bottoms, cut into
    quarters
4 baby zucchini, sliced thickly
4 garlic cloves, finely sliced
1 cup shelled fresh peas
4–6 scallions, thickly sliced
small bunch of dill, finely chopped
salt and black pepper

For the couscous

2⅔ cups couscous
½ teaspoon salt
2 cups warm water
1–2 tablespoons olive oil
1 tablespoon butter, cut into
    small pieces

- Put the couscous into an ovenproof dish. Stir the salt into the measured water and pour it over the couscous. Cover with a clean dish towel and let stand for about 10 minutes. Using your fingers, rub the oil into the grains until light, airy, and any lumps are broken up. Sprinkle with the butter and cover with a piece of damp parchment paper. Put into a preheated oven, at 350°F, for about 10–15 minutes, until heated through.

- Meanwhile, bring the stock and saffron to a boil in a heavy saucepan. Add the fava beans, artichoke bottoms, zucchini, and garlic and cook for 2–3 minutes. Add the peas and scallions, reduce the heat, and simmer for 10 minutes, until the vegetables are tender. Season and stir in the dill.

- Using a slotted spoon, remove the vegetables from the broth and arrange over the couscous in a shallow serving dish. Drizzle with a little broth and serve the remaining broth separately in a small bowl.

---

10 Speedy Herb Couscous

Put 2 cups couscous into a heatproof bowl and just cover with boiling water. Cover with plastic wrap and let stand for 5 minutes, then fluff with a fork. Stir in 2 tablespoons olive oil to separate the grains, then toss in the juice of 1 lemon and 1 tablespoon each of finely chopped flat leaf parsley, cilantro, and mint. Season and serve as a side dish.

20 Preserved Lemon and Herb Couscous

Salad Put 2 cups couscous into a bowl. Stir ½ teaspoon salt into 1¾ cups warm water and pour it over the couscous. Cover with a clean dish towel and let stand for about 10 minutes. Using your fingertips, rub 1–2 tablespoons olive oil into the grains for 4–5 minutes, until light, airy, and any lumps are broken up. Add 2–3 finely chopped scallions, 1 seeded and finely chopped green chile, the finely chopped rind of 1 preserved lemon (see page 68), and 2 tablespoons each of finely chopped flat leaf parsley, mint, and cilantro. Season, toss well, and serve.

Couscous with Orangy Fennel and Zucchini

Serves 4

2 tablespoons olive oil

1–2 teaspoons anise seeds

grated rind of 1 orange

2 fennel bulbs, trimmed and cut into quarters

juice of 2 oranges

1 zucchini, halved and sliced lengthwise

1 tablespoon butter

1 tablespoon honey

1 tablespoon orange blossom water

salt and black pepper

½ orange, thinly sliced, to garnish

For the couscous

2 cups couscous

½ teaspoon salt

1¾ cups warm water

2 tablespoons olive oil

1 tablespoon butter, cut into small pieces

- Prepare and cook the couscous following the 30-minute method on page 134.

- Meanwhile, heat the oil in a heavy skillet or the bottom of a tagine, stir in the anise seeds and orange rind and cook for 1–2 minutes, until fragrant. Toss in the fennel and coat well, then pour in the orange juice. Cover and cook gently for 3–4 minutes.

- Add the zucchini and butter, season, and drizzle the honey over the vegetables. Cover and cook for 3–4 minutes, until the vegetables are tender. Remove the lid and let simmer for 3–4 minutes, until the liquid is reduced and slightly caramelized, then pour in the orange blossom water.

- Spoon the fennel and zucchini mixture over the couscous in a shallow serving dish. Drizzle with the caramelized juice and garnish with the orange slices.

 Fennel and Onion Couscous

Put 2 cups couscous into a heatproof bowl and just cover with boiling water. Cover with plastic wrap and let stand for 5 minutes. Meanwhile, heat 1 tablespoon each of olive oil and butter in a skillet, stir in 1–2 teaspoons fennel seeds, 1 sliced red onion, and 1 trimmed and sliced fennel bulb, and cook for 4–5 minutes. Season and toss in the couscous. Serve as a side dish with lemon wedges.

Fennel, Orange, and Zahtar

Couscous Prepare and heat 2 cups couscous following the 20-minute method on page 138, omitting the lemon rind and black pepper. Meanwhile, put 2 trimmed and finely sliced fennel bulbs into a broiler pan. Drizzle with 2 tablespoons olive oil, season, and cook under a preheated hot broiler for 10 minutes, until tender and beginning to brown. Remove the peel and pith from 1 orange, then thinly slice and quarter the slices, removing any seeds. Sprinkle the orange slices over the fennel. Drizzle with 1–2 teaspoons honey and broil for another 2–3 minutes. Spoon the fennel and orange mixture over the couscous on a serving dish. Melt ½ tablespoon butter and drizzle it over the top. Sprinkle with 1–2 teaspoons zahtar and serve hot.

20 Lemon Couscous with Spicy Shellfish

Serves 6–8

2–3 tablespoons olive oil

1½ lb store-bought prepared
seafood selection

2 teaspoons harissa paste
(see page 70)

bunch of cilantro, finely chopped

salt and black pepper

For the lemon couscous

2⅔ cups couscous

2 tablespoons sunflower oil

finely chopped rind of 1 preserved
lemon (see page 68)

2 tablespoons butter, cut into
small pieces

- Put the couscous into a heatproof bowl and just cover with boiling water. Cover with plastic wrap and let stand for 5 minutes. Fluff up with a fork, then stir in the oil to separate the grains. Put into an ovenproof dish, stir in the preserved lemon rind, season with black pepper, and sprinkle with the butter. Cover with a damp piece of wax paper and put into a preheated oven, at 350°F, for 10 minutes, until heated through.

- Meanwhile, heat the olive oil in a heavy skillet, add the seafood, and cook for 3–4 minutes. Add the harissa, season, and stir in most of the cilantro.

- Spoon the seafood over the couscous in a shallow serving dish and serve garnished with the remaining cilantro.

10 Lemon Couscous with Steamed

Shellfish Cook 2⅓ cups lemon couscous according to the package directions. Meanwhile, steam 1½ lb peeled shrimp or scallops for 3–4 minutes, until opaque, then put into a bowl and add 2–3 tablespoons olive oil, the grated rind and juice of 2 limes, 2 crushed garlic cloves, 2 seeded and finely sliced green chiles, and a finely chopped small bunch of mint. Season, toss well, and serve with the couscous.

30 Lemon Couscous with Shellfish K'dra

Heat 2 tablespoons olive or argan oil in a large copper or heavy saucepan, stir in 2 teaspoons each of cumin seeds and coriander seeds, 2–3 teaspoons seeded and finely chopped red chiles, and 1–2 teaspoons sugar, and cook for 1–2 minutes, until fragrant. Stir in 2 teaspoons turmeric, 1 (14½ oz) can tomatoes, drained of juice, ⅔ cup white wine, 3½ cups hot fish stock, 4 finely sliced garlic cloves, ½ cup peeled and finely sliced fresh ginger root, and a finely chopped small

bunch each of flat leaf parsley and cilantro and bring to a boil, then reduce the heat and simmer for 15 minutes. Season and bring to a boil, then add 8 oz peeled shrimp, 8 oz fresh mussels, cleaned following the instructions in the 20-minute method on page 86, and 8 oz scallops, cover, and cook for 5–8 minutes, until the mussels open and the shrimp and scallops are opaque. Discard any mussels that remain shut. Meanwhile, prepare the Lemon Couscous as above, then serve with the shellfish and stock, garnished with chopped herbs.

Ginger and Honey Lamb and Apricot Tagine

Serves 4

1–2 tablespoons olive or argan oil
1 onion, finely chopped
2–3 garlic cloves, finely chopped
¼ cup peeled and finely chopped
   fresh ginger root
1 lb lean lamb, cut into
   bite-size pieces
2 teaspoons ground cinnamon
1⅓ cups dried apricots
2 large tablespoons honey
salt and black pepper
Buttery Couscous (see page 128),
   to serve

- Heat the oil in a large, heavy saucepan or the bottom of a tagine, stir in the onion, garlic, and ginger, and cook for 1–2 minutes. Add the lamb and toss to coat well, then add the cinnamon. Pour in enough hot water to just cover the meat and bring to a boil. Reduce the heat, cover, and simmer for 15 minutes.

- Add the apricots and honey, replace the lid, and simmer for another 10 minutes. Season to taste and serve hot with the couscous.

 Quick Ginger and Honey Lamb Heat 1–2 tablespoons ghee in a large, heavy saucepan or the bottom of a tagine, stir in 2 finely chopped garlic cloves, 2 teaspoons cumin seeds, and ¼ cup peeled and finely chopped fresh ginger root, and cook for 2 minutes. Add 1 lb cubed lamb and cook for another 5–6 minutes, until browned and cooked through. Stir in 1 tablespoon honey, season, and toss in 1 tablespoon finely chopped cilantro. Serve with couscous.

 Spicy Ginger and Honey Lamb Tagine Heat 1–2 tablespoons olive oil in a large, heavy saucepan or the bottom of a tagine, stir in 1 chopped onion, 2 chopped garlic cloves, 1–2 seeded and finely chopped red chiles, and ¼ cup peeled and chopped fresh ginger root, and cook for 1–2 minutes. Stir in 1 lb cubed lamb, 2 tablespoons honey, and enough hot water to cover. Bring to a boil, cover, and simmer for 15 minutes. Season to taste and toss in 1 tablespoon finely chopped cilantro. Serve with plain buttery couscous or a herb couscous.

1 Spicy Beef, Sun-Dried Tomatoes, and Pine Nuts

Serves 4

2 tablespoons pine nuts

2 cups cooked thin lean
   beef strips

1 cup drained and sliced
   sun-dried tomatoes in oil

2–3 tablespoons olive or argan oil

juice of 1 lemon

1 teaspoon harissa paste
   (see page 70)

bunch of flat leaf parsley, chopped

salt and black pepper

couscous, to serve (optional)

- Dry-fry the pine nuts in a small, heavy skillet over medium heat for 2 minutes, until golden brown.

- Put the beef, tomatoes, and most of the toasted pine nuts in a bowl. Mix together the oil, lemon juice, harissa, and parsley in a separate bowl and season. Pour the mixture over the beef and toss well.

- Sprinkle with the reserved pine nuts and serve with couscous, if desired.

 Turmeric Beef and Sun-Dried Tomato Tagine Heat 2 tablespoons ghee in a large saucepan or the bottom of a tagine, stir in 2 chopped garlic cloves, 2 seeded and chopped red chiles, 1 tablespoon chopped ginger root, and 1 teaspoon sugar, and cook for 2–3 minutes. Add 1 lb beef, cut into strips and tossed in 1 tablespoon turmeric, coat well, and cook for 1–2 minutes, then add ¾ cup drained and sliced sun-dried tomatoes in oil and 1 tablespoon chopped cilantro. Pour in enough water to just cover the bottom of the pan, drizzle with 2 teaspoons honey, cover, and cook for 15 minutes. Season, garnish with a little more finely chopped cilantro, and serve with chunks of crusty bread or couscous.

 Beef, Eggplant, and Sun-Dried Tomato Tagine Cut 1 eggplant into bite-size pieces, put into a colander and sprinkle with salt. Meanwhile, heat 2–3 tablespoons argan oil or ghee in a large, heavy saucepan or the bottom of a tagine, stir in 2 finely chopped onions, 4 finely chopped garlic cloves, 1–2 seeded and finely chopped red chiles, ¼ cup peeled and finely chopped fresh ginger root, and 2 teaspoons coriander seeds, and cook for 2–3 minutes. Add 1 tablespoon crumbled dried sage leaves and 1 lb lean beef, cut into bite-size pieces, and stir well to coat. Pour in 2 cups hot beef or chicken stock, bring to a boil, then reduce the heat, cover, and simmer for 10 minutes. Rinse the eggplants and pat dry, then stir into the beef, replace the lid, and cook for another 10 minutes. Add ¾ cup drained and coarsely chopped sun-dried tomatoes in oil and 1 tablespoon honey. Season, replace the lid, and continue to cook for 5 minutes. Sprinkle with a finely chopped bunch of flat leaf parsley and serve with chunks of crusty bread or couscous.

3️⃣ Chicken, Green Olive, and Preserved Lemon Tagine

Serves 4

1–2 tablespoons olive or argan oil
2 garlic cloves, finely chopped
1 onion, finely chopped
1 teaspoon coriander seeds
1 teaspoon cumin seeds
8 chicken thighs
juice of 1 lemon
pinch of saffron threads
2 cinnamon sticks
2 tablespoons butter
rind of 1 preserved lemon, cut
    into thin strips (see page 68)
1¾ cups cracked green olives
salt and black pepper
Buttery Couscous (see page 128),
    to serve (optional)

- Heat the oil in a large, heavy saucepan or the bottom of a tagine, stir in the garlic, onion, and coriander and cumin seeds, and cook for 1–2 minutes. Add the chicken thighs and lightly brown on each side.

- Pour in the lemon juice and enough water to just cover the chicken. Stir in the saffron, cinnamon sticks, and butter and bring to a boil, then reduce the heat, cover, and simmer for 15 minutes.

- Add the preserved lemon rind and olives, replace the lid, and simmer for another 10 minutes. Season to taste and serve hot with the couscous, if desired.

 Spicy Chicken and Preserved Lemon Pittas Heat 2 tablespoons olive oil and a pat of butter in a skillet or tagine, stir in 2 crushed garlic cloves, and cook for 1 minute, then stir in 1–2 teaspoons harissa paste (see page 70) and 1¾–2½ cups cooked chicken strips tossed with 2 teaspoons turmeric. Heat through, then add 1 tablespoon chopped preserved lemon rind (see page 68) and 1 tablespoon chopped cilantro. Season and spoon into 4 pita breads. Serve with dollops of plain yogurt and a sprinkling of chopped flat leaf parsley.

 Spicy Chicken and Preserved Lemon Tagine Heat 1–2 tablespoons olive oil in a large, heavy saucepan or the bottom of a tagine, stir in 2 finely chopped garlic cloves, 1 finely chopped onion, 1 seeded and finely chopped red chile, and 2 teaspoons coriander seeds, and cook for 1–2 minutes. Toss in 1 lb diced or sliced skinless, boneless chicken breasts and cook for 2–3 minutes, until browned, then pour in ½ cup white wine and enough water to just cover the chicken and bring to a boil. Reduce the heat, cover, and simmer for 10 minutes. Add the finely chopped rind of 1 preserved lemon (see page 68), replace the lid, and simmer for another 5 minutes, until the chicken is cooked through. Season to taste and serve sprinkled with 1 tablespoon finely chopped flat leaf parsley. Serve with a herb couscous.

20 Chermoula Monkfish and Black Olive Tagine

Serves 4

1¼ lb monkfish tail, cut into bite-size pieces
2 tablespoons prepared chermoula paste
2 tablesoons olive oil
2 tablespoons marinated black ripe olives, drained and pitted
¼ cup fino sherry
salt and black pepper

To garnish
smoked paprika
finely chopped flat leaf parsley

- Place the monkfish tail in a bowl, rub with the chermoula, and let marinate for 5 minutes.

- Heat the oil in a heavy skillet or the bottom of a tagine, stir in the monkfish, olives, and sherry, cover, and cook for 10–15 minutes, until the fish is cooked through. Season, then serve sprinkled with a little paprika and parsley.

 Steamed Monkfish with Chermoula and Couscous Line a steamer with cilantro leaves and place 1¼ lb monkfish tail, cut into bite-size pieces, on top. Steam for 8–10 minutes, until just cooked through and tender. Season and serve hot with a bowl of prepared chermoula paste for dipping. Serve with a herb or spicy couscous.

 Monkfish, Potato, and Chermoula Tagine Using a mortar and pestle, pound 1 garlic clove and 1 teaspoon sea salt to a smooth paste. Stir in 2 teaspoons ground cumin, 1–2 teaspoons smoked paprika, the juice of 1 lemon, and a coarsely chopped small bunch of cilantro, then mix with 2 tablespoons olive oil. Reserve 1 tablespoon, then rub the rest over 1¼ lb monkfish and let marinate for at least 10 minutes to let the flavors mingle. Meanwhile, parboil 8 peeled new potatoes in a saucepan of boiling water for 6–8 minutes, or until slightly softened. Drain, refresh under cold running water, and cut in half lengthwise. Heat 1 tablespoon olive oil in a skillet or the bottom of a tagine, stir in 1 crushed garlic clove, and cook until it begins to brown, then add the potatoes and the reserved chermoula and season. Top with the marinated fish, sprinkle with 10–12 cherry tomatoes, and drizzle with 1 tablespoon olive oil. Pour in ½ cup water, cover, and cook over medium heat for 10–15 minutes, until cooked through. Season and gently stir together. Serve immediately with warm crusty bread to mop up the juices.

30 Lamb, Sweet Potato, and Okra K'dra

Serves 6–8

2 tablespoons smen or ghee

3 onions, finely sliced

2–3 teaspoons coriander seeds

2–3 cinnamon sticks

1 teaspoon black peppercorns

pinch of saffron threads

1 lb lean lamb, cut into
   bite-size pieces

5 cups hot lamb or chicken stock

2 sweet potatoes, peeled and
   cut into bite-size pieces

1 tablespoon butter

8 oz fresh okra

juice of 1 lemon

salt

couscous, to serve (optional)

- Heat the smen or ghee in a large copper or heavy saucepan, stir in the onions, and cook for 1–2 minutes. Add the coriander seeds, cinnamon sticks, peppercorns, saffron, and lamb and mix well.

- Pour in the stock and bring to a boil, then cover, reduce the heat, and cook gently for 10 minutes. Add the sweet potatoes and butter, replace the lid, and cook gently for another 10 minutes.

- Meanwhile, place the okra in a nonmetallic bowl, pour the lemon juice over them, and let stand for 10 minutes, then drain.

- Add the okra to the pan and simmer for another 5–8 minutes, until cooked through but still retaining a crunch. Season with salt. Serve the lamb and vegetables with couscous, if desired, pouring the sauce into a bowl to serve separately.

---

10 Buttered Okra with Preserved Lemon

Put 1 lb okra in a nonmetallic bowl, pour the juice of 2 lemons over them, and let stand for 3–4 minutes, then drain well. Heat 2 tablespoons olive oil in a heavy skillet or the bottom of a tagine, add the okra, and cook for 4–5 minutes. Stir in the sliced rind of 1 preserved lemon (see page 68) and season. Pour 1 tablespoon melted butter over the top and serve with plain buttery couscous.

20 Quick Lamb, Lemon, and Okra

K'dra Heat 2 tablespoons smen or ghee in a large copper or heavy saucepan, stir in 3 finely sliced onions, 2 teaspoons coriander seeds, 2 cinnamon sticks, and a pinch of saffron threads, and cook for 2–3 minutes. Add 1 lb lean lamb, cut into thin strips, mix well, and add 1 lemon, cut into 6 segments. Pour in 3½ cups hot lamb or chicken stock, cover, and cook over medium heat for

12–15 minutes, until cooked through. Meanwhile, put 8 oz fresh okra in a nonmetallic bowl, pour the juice of 1 lemon over them, and let stand for 5 minutes, then drain. Add to the lamb 5 minutes before the end of the cooking time. Season and stir in a coarsely chopped small bunch of flat leaf parsley. Serve with couscous, pouring the sauce into a bowl to serve with it.

3⏱ Beef, Prune, and Almond Tagine

Serves 4

1–2 tablespoons ghee
1 onion, finely chopped
2–3 garlic cloves, finely chopped
¼ cup peeled and finely chopped
fresh ginger root
1 lb lean beef, cut into
bite-size pieces
1–2 teaspoons ras el hanout
1½ cups pitted dried prunes
1 cup blanched almonds
2 tablespoons honey
salt and black pepper
finely chopped flat leaf parsley,
to garnish
Buttery Couscous (see page 128),
to serve

- Heat the ghee in a large, heavy saucepan or the bottom of a tagine, stir in the onion, garlic, and ginger, and cook for 1–2 minutes. Add the beef and coat well, then add the ras el hanout.

- Pour in enough water to just cover the meat and bring to a boil. Reduce the heat, cover, and simmer for 15 minutes.

- Add the prunes and almonds and stir in the honey. Season, bring back to a boil, replace the lid, and cook over medium heat for another 10 minutes. Garnish with parsley and serve with couscous.

1⏱ Almond-Stuffed Prunes in Orange

Syrup Open up 12 pitted dried prunes and stuff each one with a blanched almond. Place the prunes in a skillet or the bottom of a tagine, pour the juice of 2 oranges and 2 tablespoons orange blossom water over them, and drizzle with 1 tablespoon honey. Bring to a boil, cover, and cook over medium heat for 8–9 minutes. Baste the prunes in the syrupy juice, dust with 1 teaspoon ground cinnamon, and serve with tagines and couscous.

2⏱ Almond and Ginger Beef Tagine

Heat 1–2 tablespoons ghee in a large, heavy saucepan or the bottom of a tagine, stir in 2 finely chopped garlic cloves, 2 teaspoons coriander seeds, 1 teaspoon finely chopped dried red chile, and ½ cup peeled and finely chopped fresh ginger root, and cook for 1–2 minutes. Add 1 lb lean beef, cut into thin strips, mix well, and cook for 2–3 minutes. Add 1 cup sliced blanched almonds, 1 tablespoon honey, and 1¾ cups water and bring to a boil, then cover and cook over medium heat for 15 minutes. Season, garnish with a finely chopped small bunch of cilantro, and serve with couscous.

MOR-COUS-HUB

30 Meatball and Egg Tagine with Toasted Cumin

Serves 4

2½ cups water
1 tablespoon butter
1 teaspoon salt
½ teaspoon cayenne powder
4 eggs
1–2 teaspoons cumin seeds
small bunch of flat leaf parsley,
   finely chopped, to garnish
buttered toasted flatbreads,
   to serve (optional)

For the meatballs

8 oz lean ground lamb
1 onion, finely chopped
1–2 teaspoons dried mint
1–2 teaspoons ground cinnamon
1–2 teaspoons ras el hanout
salt and black pepper

- To make the meatballs, mix together all the ingredients in a bowl and season. Knead the mixture well, then roll cherry-size pieces into firm balls. Pour the measured water into a large saucepan or the bottom of a tagine and bring to a boil. Add the meatballs, a few at a time, and poach for about 10 minutes, turning occasionally, until cooked through. Remove with a slotted spoon and drain on paper towels.

- Pour about ½ cup of the cooking liquid into a saucepan or the bottom of a tagine and bring to a boil. Stir in the butter, salt, and cayenne, then add the meatballs. Make 4 wells, then break the eggs into the wells, cover, and cook for 5–6 minutes, until the whites are just set but the yolks are still runny.

- Meanwhile, dry-fry the cumin seeds in a small, heavy skillet over medium heat for 1–2 minutes, until they emit a nutty aroma. Put into a spice grinder and grind over the eggs. Garnish with the parsley and serve immediately, with buttered toasted flatbreads, if desired.

---

10 Eggs with Toasted Cumin

Heat 1 tablespoon ghee in a large, heavy skillet or the bottom of a tagine, break in 6–8 eggs, and sprinkle with a little paprika and salt. Cover and cook gently until the whites are firm. Meanwhile, dry-fry 1–2 teaspoons cumin seeds as above. Place in a spice grinder and grind over the eggs. Serve with buttered toasted flatbreads.

20 Meatball, Toasted Cumin, and Egg

Tagine Mix together 8 oz lean ground lamb, 1 finely chopped onion, 1 tablespoon finely chopped parsley, and 1–2 teaspoons ras el hanout in a bowl and season. Knead and shape the mixture as above. Heat 1–2 tablespoons ghee in a heavy skillet or the bottom of a tagine, stir in 2 teaspoons cumin seeds, toasted as above, and cook for 1 minute. Add the meatballs and cook for 2–3 minutes, then pour in 1¼ cups water and season. Bring to a boil, cover, and cook over medium heat for 10–12 minutes, until cooked through. Meanwhile, soft-boil 2 eggs, then drain, shell, and coarsely chop. Sprinkle them over the meatballs, garnish with a finely chopped small bunch of cilantro, and serve with couscous.

20 Toasted Saffron, Herb, and Preserved Lemon Fish Tagine

Serves 4

pinch of saffron threads
1¼ cups warm water
1–2 tablespoons olive oil
finely sliced rind of 1 preserved
   lemon (see page 68)
1 lb skinless firm fish fillets,
   such as sea bass or halibut,
   cut into chunks
small bunch of mint,
   finely chopped
salt and black pepper
couscous, to serve (optional)

- Dry-fry the saffron in a small skillet over medium heat for less than a minute, until it emits a faint aroma. Using a mortar and pestle or spice grinder, grind to a powder, then stir in the measured water until the saffron dissolves.

- Heat the oil in a heavy saucepan or the bottom of a tagine, stir in the preserved lemon rind, fish, most of the mint, and the saffron water, and bring to a boil. Season, cover, and cook gently, stirring occasionally, for 15 minutes, until the fish is cooked through. Garnish with the reserved mint and serve with couscous, if desired.

---

10 Sea Bass with Olives, Saffron, and Preserved Lemon

Heat 2 tablespoons olive oil in a heavy saucepan or the bottom of a tagine, stir in a pinch of saffron threads, 2 tablespoons finely sliced green olives, and 1 tablespoon finely sliced preserved lemon rind (see page 68) and cook for 1–2 minutes. Add 1 lb skinless firm fish fillets, such as sea bass or halbut, cut into bite-size pieces, and cook for another 2–3 minutes. Season, cover, and cook over low heat for 5 minutes, until the fish is just cooked through. Serve with couscous.

30 Toasted Saffron, Preserved Lemon, Potato, and Fish Tagine

Parboil 1 lb new potatoes in a saucepan of boiling water for about 8 minutes or until slightly softened. Meanwhile, dry-fry and grind a pinch of saffron threads as above, then stir in ⅔ cup warm water until the saffron dissolves. Set aside. Cut 4 tomatoes into slices. Drain the potatoes, then refresh under cold running water and peel off the skins. Cut into thick slices. Heat 2 tablespoons olive oil in a large, heavy saucepan or the bottom of a tagine, stir in 4–6 peeled and smashed garlic cloves, and cook for 1–2 minutes, until beginning to brown. Reduce the heat to low and line the pan with the potatoes, followed by a layer of the tomatoes, reserving a few slices. Sprinkle with the finely sliced rind of ½ preserved lemon (see page 68) and ½ finely chopped small bunch of flat leaf parsley and top with 1 lb sea bass fillets, skinned and cut into chunks. Mix together the saffron water, the juice of 1 lemon, and 1 tablespoon olive oil and season well. Pour the sauce over the fish, top with the reserved tomatoes, and sprinkle with another layer of preserved lemon rind and parsley. Cover and cook over medium heat for 15 minutes, until the fish is just cooked through. Serve immediately with couscous.

30 Herbed Shrimp, Tomato, and Turmeric Fennel Tagine

Serves 4

2 fennel bulbs, trimmed and
  thickly sliced lengthwise
3 tablespoons olive oil
1 tablespoon butter
2–3 teaspoons turmeric
1 onion, finely chopped
2 garlic cloves, finely chopped
¼ cup peeled and finely chopped
  fresh ginger root
1 lb peeled shrimp
1 teaspoon smoked paprika
1 teaspoon sugar
1 (14½ oz) can tomatoes,
  drained of juice
small bunch of cilantro, chopped
bunch of flat leaf parsley, chopped
salt and black pepper
chunks of crusty bread or
  couscous, to serve (optional)

- Place the fennel in a steamer basket and steam for 5–6 minutes to soften. Refresh under cold running water, drain, and pat dry. Heat 1 tablespoon of the oil and the butter in a heavy skillet, add the fennel, and cook for 3–4 minutes on each side, until golden brown. Toss in 1–2 teaspoons of the turmeric and set aside.

- Heat the remaining oil in a large, heavy skillet or the bottom of a tagine, stir in the onion, garlic, and ginger, and cook for 1–2 minutes, until beginning to brown. Add the shrimp and cook for 2–3 minutes, until they turn pink, then stir in the remaining turmeric and the paprika. Add the sugar, tomatoes, and half the herbs. Cover and cook gently for 10 minutes.

- Gently stir in the fennel, replace the lid, and cook for another 5 minutes. Season, garnish with the remaining herbs, and serve with crusty bread or couscous, if desired.

 Spicy Turmeric and Lime Shrimp
Heat 2 tablespoons olive oil in a skillet or tagine, stir in 2 chopped garlic cloves, 1–2 seeded and chopped chiles, and 1 tablespoon chopped preserved lemon rind (see page 68), and cook for 1–2 minutes. Stir in 1 lb peeled shrimp and cook for 2–3 minutes. Stir in 2 teaspoons turmeric and the juice of 2 limes, heat, and season. Garnish with a chopped bunch of cilantro and serve with warm flatbreads or couscous.

 Turmeric Shrimp, Fennel, and Tomato Tagine Heat 2–3 tablespoons olive oil in a heavy saucepan or the bottom of a tagine, add 1 lb peeled shrimp, and cook for 2–3 minutes, until they turn pink. Remove from the heat, toss in 1–2 teaspoons turmeric, then drain on paper towels. Stir 2 finely chopped garlic cloves and ¼ cup peeled and finely chopped fresh ginger root into the pan and cook for 1–2 minutes, then add 2 finely sliced fennel bulbs and cook for another 2 minutes to soften. Add 1 teaspoon sugar, 1 (14½ oz) can tomatoes, drained of juice, and ½ cup white wine. Cover and cook over medium heat for 10 minutes. Season and stir in the shrimp. Garnish with 1 tablespoon finely chopped cilantro and serve with chunks of crusty bread or couscous.

30 Cinnamon Duck and Caramelized Pear Tagine

Serves 4

2 tablespoons olive oil

2 onions, finely chopped

¼ cup peeled and finely chopped
fresh ginger root

2 cinnamon sticks

pinch of saffron threads

1 lb duck breasts, cubed

1¾ cups hot chicken stock

2 tablespoons butter

3–¼ cup honey

2 pears, peeled, quartered,
and cored

2–3 tablespoons orange
blossom water

salt and black pepper

a few shredded lemon balm or
mint leaves, to garnish

Buttery Couscous (see page 128),
to serve

- Heat the oil in a heavy skillet or the bottom of a tagine, stir in the onions and ginger, and cook until they begin to brown, then add the cinnamon sticks and saffron. Add the duck meat and coat well. Pour in the stock and bring to a boil. Reduce the heat, cover, and cook over medium heat for 20 minutes.

- Meanwhile, melt the butter in a heavy skillet and stir in the honey. Toss in the pears and cook until they begin to caramelize.

- Add the pears to the duck with the orange blossom water and cook for another 5 minutes. Season, garnish with the lemon balm or mint, and serve with couscous.

1 Spiced Duck and Prunes with Cinnamon

Cinnamon Heat 2 tablespoons butter in a skillet or tagine, stir in 1–2 teaspoons coriander seeds, 1 tablespoon chopped fresh ginger root, and ¾ cup sliced pitted prunes, and cook for 2 minutes. Add 2½ cups cooked duck strips, 1 tablespoon honey, and 2–3 tablespoons orange blossom water, cover, and cook over medium heat for 6–8 minutes, until heated through. Season, dust with cinnamon, and serve with some couscous.

2 Duck, Plum, and Cinnamon Tagine

Place 6–8 halved and pitted ripe red or purple plums in a blender and process to a puree. Heat 2 tablespoons olive oil and a pat of butter in a heavy skillet or the bottom of a tagine and stir in 2–3 cinnamon sticks, 6 cloves, and 1 teaspoon each of cumin seeds and cardamom seeds. Add 1 lb sliced duck breasts and cook for 2–3 minutes, stirring to coat well, then add 1 tablespoon honey and the pureed plums. Cover and cook over medium heat for 12–15 minutes, until cooked through. Season, garnish with a dusting of confectioners' sugar, followed by a dusting of ground cinnamon, and serve with couscous.

Cardamom Lamb and Dates

Serves 4

2 tablespoons ghee
2 red chiles, seeded and
  finely sliced
2 garlic cloves, finely chopped
2 teaspoons cardamom seeds
2½ cups cubed cooked lamb
2–3 tablespoons coarsely
  chopped dried dates
1 tablespoon honey
juice of 1 lemon
salt and black pepper
finely chopped rind of ½ preserved
  lemon (see page 68), to garnish
flatbreads or couscous, to serve
  (optional)

- Heat the ghee in a heavy skillet or the bottom of a tagine, stir in the chiles, garlic, and cardamom seeds, and cook for 1–2 minutes, until they begin to brown. Add the lamb and cook for 2 minutes.

- Add the dates, honey, and lemon juice and season. Cover and cook gently for 5–6 minutes, until heated through. Garnish with the preserved lemon rind and serve with flatbreads or couscous, if desired.

---

2 **Date, Cardamom, and Caramelized Shallot Tagine** Heat 1–2 tablespoons ghee in a skillet or the bottom of a tagine, stir in 2 teaspoons cardamom seeds and 2–3 cinnamon sticks, and cook for 1 minute. Toss in 12–16 peeled shallots and cook, stirring, for 2–3 minutes, until they begin to brown. Stir in 2 tablespoons honey, 2 cups pitted dates, and the juice of 1 lemon and season. Cover and cook gently for 15 minutes, until the shallots are caramelized. Garnish with the sliced rind of ½ preserved lemon (see page 68) and serve as a side dish.

3 **Date, Shallot, and Cardamom Lamb Tagine** Heat 2 tablespoons ghee in a heavy saucepan or the bottom of a tagine, add 1 lb lean lamb, cut into bite-size pieces, and cook for 1–2 minutes, until browned. Remove the lamb with a slotted spoon and set aside. Stir in 12 shallots and 4 halved garlic cloves and cook for 2–3 minutes, until they begin to brown. Add 2 teaspoons turmeric, 8 cardamom pods, and 2 cinnamon sticks and the lamb. Pour in enough water or meat stock to just cover and bring to a boil. Cover, reduce the heat, and cook gently for 15 minutes.

Stir in 1–2 tablespoons honey, season, and add 2 cups pitted dates, replace the lid, and cook over medium heat for 10 minutes. Garnish with the finely sliced rind of ½ preserved lemon (see page 68) and serve with chunks of crusty bread or couscous.

30 Chorizo, Lentil, and Fenugreek Tagine

Serves 4

2 tablespoons argan oil or ghee
2 onions, coarsely chopped
4 garlic cloves, coarsely chopped
1 lb chorizo sausage, thickly sliced
2 teaspoons turmeric
2 teaspoons ground fenugreek
1 cup brown dried lentils, rinsed,
    picked over, and drained
1 (14½ oz) can diced tomatoes
2 teaspoons sugar
small bunch of cilantro, chopped
salt and black pepper

To serve

toasted flatbreads
plain yogurt

- Heat the oil in a heavy saucepan or the bottom of a tagine, stir in the onions and garlic, and cook for 1–2 minutes, until they begin to brown. Toss in the chorizo and cook for 1–2 minutes to flavor the oil. Add the turmeric, fenugreek, and lentils and stir to coat well.

- Add the tomatoes and sugar and pour in enough water to cover the lentils by 1 inch. Bring to a boil, then cover, reduce the heat, and cook gently for about 25 minutes, until the lentils are tender but not mushy, adding more water if necessary.

- Stir in most of the cilantro and season. Garnish with the remaining cilantro and serve with toasted flatbreads and dollops of yogurt.

---

10 Chorizo and Raisins with Fenugreek

Heat 1–2 tablespoons ghee in a saucepan or tagine, stir in 2 teaspoons coriander seeds, 2 sliced onions, and 1 teaspoon sugar, and cook for 2–3 minutes. Toss in 2 tablespoons raisins, 1 lb sliced chorizo, and 1 teaspoon ground fenugreek. Cover and cook over medium heat for 4–5 minutes. Season and stir in the chopped rind of ½ preserved lemon (see page 68). Garnish with a chopped bunch of flat leaf parsley and serve with toasted flatbreads and dollops of yogurt.

20 Chorizo, Potato, and Fenugreek

Tagine Heat 2 tablespoons argan oil or ghee in a heavy saucepan or the bottom of a tagine, stir in 2–3 crushed garlic cloves and 2 teaspoons coriander seeds, and cook for 1 minute. Add 8 oz thickly sliced chorizo and cook for 1–2 minutes to flavor the oil. Stir in 1 teaspoon turmeric, 2 teaspoons ground fenugreek, and 12 peeled small potatoes and coat well in the oil. Drizzle with 1 tablespoon honey and pour in enough water to just cover the potatoes. Bring to a boil, then season, cover, and cook over medium heat for 15 minutes, until the potatoes are tender. Garnish with coarsely chopped cilantro and serve with a salad or couscous.

30 Herbed Carrot, Potato, and Pea Tagine

Serves 4

2–3 tablespoons olive or argan oil

2 onions, sliced

4 garlic cloves, chopped

¼ cup peeled and chopped fresh ginger root

1–2 red chiles, seeded and chopped

1 teaspoon cumin seeds

1–2 teaspoons turmeric

1 teaspoon paprika

8 small potatoes, peeled

3–4 carrots, peeled and each cut into 3–4 chunks

2½ cups hot vegetable or chicken stock

1½ cups fresh or frozen peas

small bunch of flat leaf parsley, finely chopped

small bunch of mint, finely chopped

3–4 tomatoes, sliced

1½ tablespoons butter, cubed

salt and black pepper

couscous, to serve (optional)

- Heat the oil in a heavy saucepan or the bottom of a tagine, stir in the onions, garlic, ginger, chiles, and cumin seeds, and cook for 2–3 minutes. Add the turmeric and paprika and toss in the potatoes and carrots.

- Pour in the stock and bring to a boil. Cover, reduce the heat, and cook gently for 15 minutes, until the vegetables are tender.

- Stir in the peas and half the herbs. Season and top with the tomato slices. Sprinkle with the butter and remaining herbs. Replace the lid and cook for another 5–10 minutes. Serve with couscous, if desired.

10 Preserved Lemon and Sage Carrots

Heat 1 tablespoon olive oil and 2 tablespoons butter in a skillet or tagine, stir in 2–3 peeled and sliced carrots, the sliced rind of 1 preserved lemon (see page 68), and a pinch of dried sage. Cover and cook over medium heat for 8–10 minutes, until just tender. Season and serve with tagines.

20 Carrot, Potato, and Sage Tagine

Heat 2 tablespoons argan oil or ghee in a heavy skillet or the bottom of a tagine, stir in 2–3 crushed garlic cloves, 1 teaspoon coriander seeds, and 1 tablespoon crumbled dried sage, and cook for 1–2 minutes. Toss in 2 peeled and thickly sliced carrots and 4 peeled and thickly sliced potatoes. Stir in 2 teaspoons turmeric, 1 teaspoon smoked paprika, 1 tablespoon honey, and the juice of 2 lemons. Season, replace the lid, and cook gently for 15 minutes, until the vegetables are tender. Serve as a side dish.

Three Bell Pepper, Olive, Feta, and Egg Tagine

Serves 4

2 tablespoons olive oil

1 teaspoon cumin seeds

1 teaspoon coriander seeds

1 each green, red, and yellow bell pepper, all cored, seeded, and finely sliced

2 tablespoons pitted and halved black ripe olives

5 oz feta cheese, cubed

4 eggs

black pepper

shredded basil leaves, to garnish

chunks of warm crusty bread, to serve (optional)

- Heat the oil in a heavy skillet or the bottom of a tagine, stir in the cumin and coriander seeds, and cook for 1–2 minutes. Add the bell peppers and cook for another 2–3 minutes, then stir in the olives. Cover, reduce the heat, and cook over medium heat for 5 minutes, until the peppers have softened.

- Add the feta and cook for 2–3 minutes, until it begins to soften, then make 4 wells in the mixture. Break the eggs into the wells, cover, and cook for 4–5 minutes, until the whites are firm. Grind black pepper over the eggs, garnish with the basil leaves, and serve with warm crusty bread, if desired.

---

1 **Spiced Tomatoes and Eggs with Roasted Red Peppers**

Heat 1–2 tablespoons ghee in a heavy skillet or the bottom of a tagine, stir in 1 teaspoon each of coriander seeds and cumin seeds and 2 crushed garlic cloves, and cook for 1–2 minutes. Top with 3–4 sliced tomatoes, then break over 8 eggs. Cover and cook over medium heat for 6–8 minutes, until the eggs are firm. Season, garnish with roasted red peppers from a jar, sliced, and sprinkle with a chopped small bunch of flat leaf parsley. Serve on buttered, toasted flatbreads.

---

3 **Bell Pepper, Tomato, and Egg Tagine** Heat 2 tablespoons ghee in a heavy skillet or the bottom of a tagine, stir in 2–3 chopped garlic cloves, 1–2 teaspoons coriander seeds, 1 teaspoon cumin seeds, and 2 seeded and finely sliced red chiles, and cook for 2 minutes. Add 2 finely sliced onions and 2 cored, seeded, and finely sliced red or green bell peppers and cook for 2–3 minutes to soften, then stir in 1–2 teaspoons sugar and 1 (14½ oz) can diced tomatoes. Cover and cook over medium heat for 15–20 minutes, until thickened. Make 4–6 wells in the mixture, then break 4–6 eggs into the wells, replace the lid, and cook gently for 4–5 minutes, until the whites are firm. Sprinkle with a finely chopped small bunch of flat leaf parsley and serve with dollops of yogurt and chunks of crusty bread.

30 Spicy Zucchini, Eggplant, and Date Tagine

Serves 4

3–¼ cup olive oil
2–3 garlic cloves, chopped
1 onion, sliced
1 red bell pepper, cored, seeded, and sliced
1 eggplant, halved and sliced
2 zucchini, sliced
2 cups pitted dates, halved lengthwise
2–3 teaspoons ras el hanout
2 teaspoons sugar
1 (28 oz) can diced tomatoes
bunch of flat leaf parsley, chopped
small bunch of cilantro, chopped
salt and black pepper

To serve

plain yogurt
chunks of crusty bread

- Heat the oil in a heavy skillet or the bottom of a tagine, stir in the garlic, onion, and red bell pepper, and cook for 1 minute, then add the eggplant and zucchini and cook for another 2 minutes.

- Add the dates, ras el hanout, sugar, tomatoes, and half the herbs and heat until simmering for 2 minutes. Cover and cook over medium heat for 25 minutes.

- Season, garnish with the remaining herbs, and serve with dollops of yogurt and crusty bread.

---

1 Spicy Zucchini, Apricots, and Dates Heat 2 tablespoons olive oil and a pat of butter in a skillet or tagine, stir in 2–3 sliced zucchini, and cook for 4–5 minutes. Slice and add 1 tablespoon each of dried apricots and pitted dates with 1 teaspoon dried red chile and 2 tablespoons orange blossom water. Season, cover, and cook for another 4–5 minutes. Garnish with the sliced rind of ½ preserved lemon (see page 68) and serve as a side dish.

2 Ras el Hanout Zucchini and Eggplant Tagine Heat ¼ cup olive or argan oil in a heavy skillet or the bottom of a tagine, stir in 2–3 crushed garlic cloves, and cook for 1 minute. Add 1 diced eggplant and 2 diced zucchini and cook for 2–3 minutes to soften. Add 2 teaspoons ras el hanout, 2 teaspoons sugar, 1 tablespoon finely chopped cilantro, and 1 (14½ oz) can diced tomatoes. Bring to a boil, then cover and cook over medium heat for 15 minutes. Garnish with a little more finely chopped cilantro mixed with the finely chopped rind of ½ preserved lemon (see page 68) and serve as a side dish.

Simple Harissa Beans

Serves 4

2 tablespoons olive oil

2 garlic cloves, finely chopped

1 finely chopped onion

2 teaspoons cumin seeds

1 teaspoon sugar

2 teaspoons harissa paste
  (see page 70)

1 (15 oz) can kidney beans,
  rinsed and drained

juice of 1 lemon

small bunch of cilantro,
  finely chopped

salt and black pepper

- Heat the oil in a heavy skillet or the bottom of a tagine, stir in the garlic, onion, cumin seeds, and sugar, and cook for 2–3 minutes, until they begin to brown.

- Add the harissa, kidney beans, and lemon juice, cover, and cook gently for 4–5 minutes, until heated through. Season and stir in the cilantro. Serve as a side dish.

Harissa, Bean, and Olive Tagine

Heat 2 tablespoons olive oil in a skillet or tagine, stir in 2 chopped garlic cloves, the sliced rind of 1 preserved lemon (see page 68), and 1 teaspoon coriander seeds and cook for 1–2 minutes. Add 1 (15 oz) can lima beans, rinsed and drained, and mix well, then add 2 tablespoons pitted black ripe olives. Stir in 1 teaspoon sugar, 1–2 teaspoons harissa paste (see page 70), and 1 (14½ oz) can diced tomatoes. Bring to a boil, then cover and cook over medium heat for 15 minutes. Season and stir in a chopped bunch each of flat leaf parsley and mint. Garnish with more chopped mint and serve with crusty bread.

Harissa Bean Tagine

Heat 2 tablespoons ghee or olive oil with a pat of butter in a heavy skillet or the bottom of a tagine, stir in 2 finely chopped garlic cloves and 1 finely chopped onion, and cook for 2–3 minutes. Add 1 teaspoon each of ground fenugreek and sugar and stir in 1–2 teaspoons harissa paste (see page 70) and 2 teaspoons tomato paste. Toss in 1 (15 oz) can navy or cannellini beans, rinsed and drained, and mix well. Pour in just enough water to cover the beans, bring to a boil, cover, and cook over a gentle heat for 25 minutes, or until tender. Season, toss in half of a finely chopped small bunch each of flat leaf parsley and cilantro and garnish with the rest. Serve with yogurt, pickles, and flatbreads.

10 Ras el Hanout Lentils and Chickpeas

Serves 4

2 tablespoons ghee or butter
2 garlic cloves, crushed
1 tablespoon peeled and finely
   chopped fresh ginger root
1¼ cups cooked brown lentils
1 cup rinsed and drained
   canned chickpeas
2 tablespoons pine nuts
1 teaspoon ras el hanout
small bunch of cilantro,
   finely chopped
salt
couscous, to serve

- Heat 1 tablespoon of the ghee or butter in a heavy skillet or the bottom of a tagine, stir in the garlic and ginger, and cook for 2 minutes. Add the lentils and chickpeas and cook for another 2–3 minutes, then season with salt.

- Meanwhile, in a separate heavy skillet, dry-fry the pine nuts over medium heat for 2–3 minutes, until they emit a nutty aroma. Stir in the remaining ghee or butter and the ras el hanout.

- Pour the pine nut mixture over the lentils and chickpeas, toss well, and sprinkle with the cilantro. Serve spooned over couscous as a side dish.

---

 2 Green Lentil and Ras el Hanout Tagine Heat 2 tablespoons ghee or argan oil in a heavy skillet or the bottom of a tagine, stir in 2–3 crushed garlic cloves and 1 teaspoon caraway seeds, and cook for 1 minute. Stir in 1 finely chopped onion, 1 peeled and finely diced carrot, and 1 teaspoon sugar and cook for 2–3 minutes. Add 1–2 teaspoons ras el hanout and 1 cup green dried lentils that have been soaked for at least 6 hours and drained. Pour in enough water to cover the lentils by 1 inch and bring to a boil. Cover and cook over medium heat for 15 minutes, until the water has been absorbed and the lentils are tender. Season well, garnish with a finely chopped small bunch of flat leaf parsley, and serve with yogurt and pickles.

 3 Lentil, Ginger, and Ras el Hanout Tagine Heat 2 tablespoons ghee in a skillet or tagine, stir in 1 chopped onion, 4 chopped garlic cloves, and ½ cup peeled and chopped fresh ginger root, and cook for 2–3 minutes. Stir in 2–3 teaspoons ras el hanout, 1 teaspoon sugar, and 1¼ cup brown dried lentils, picked over, rinsed, and drained, and mix well. Add 3 cups hot water, stir well, and bring to a boil. Cover, reduce the heat, and cook gently for 25 minutes, until all the liquid has been absorbed and the lentils are tender. Season, stir in a little of a bunch of cilantro, then garnish with the rest. Serve with yogurt and pickles or preserves.

30 Saffron, Onion, Chicken, Turnip, and Chickpea K'dra

Serves 6–8

2–3 tablespoons smen or ghee
4 onions, finely chopped
2 teaspoons cumin seeds
2–3 cinnamon sticks
pinch of saffron threads
12 chicken thighs, skinned
1 (15 oz) canned chickpeas,
   rinsed and drained
5 cups hot chicken stock
3 peeled turnips, cut into
   bite-size chunks
2 tablespoons golden raisins
1 teaspoon sea salt
1 teaspoon freshly ground
   black pepper
½ tablespoon butter
bunch of flat leaf parsley,
   finely chopped
couscous, to serve (optional)

- Heat the smen or ghee in a large copper or heavy saucepan, stir in the onions, cumin seeds, cinnamon sticks, and saffron, and cook for 1–2 minutes. Add the chicken and coat well, then add the chickpeas. Pour in the stock and bring to a boil, then reduce the heat and cook over medium heat for 15 minutes.

- Add the turnips and golden raisins, replace the lid, and cook over medium heat for another 10 minutes, until the chicken is cooked through. Season with the salt and black pepper and stir in the butter and parsley. Serve the chicken, chickpeas, and turnip with couscous, if desired, pouring the sauce into a bowl to serve separately.

1 Saffron Onions and Golden Raisins

Heat 1–2 tablespoons smen or ghee in a heavy saucepan or the bottom of a tagine, stir in 3–4 finely sliced or chopped onions, and cook for 1–2 minutes to soften. Add 2 tablespoons golden raisins and a pinch of saffron threads, cover, and cook gently for 8 minutes. Season with a little salt and serve the onion mixture as a side dish with k'dras or couscous.

2 Quick Saffron, Onion, Golden Raisin, and Chicken K'dra with Spicy Couscous

Heat 2 tablespoons smen or ghee in a large copper or heavy saucepan, stir in 3 finely sliced onions, 2 seeded and finely sliced red chiles, 2 teaspoons coriander seeds, and a pinch of saffron threads, and cook for 2–3 minutes. Add 1 lb finely sliced or diced chicken breasts and mix well, then stir in 2 tablespoons golden raisins. Pour in enough chicken stock to just cover the chicken and bring to a boil. Cover and cook over medium heat for 15 minutes, until the chicken is cooked through. Season and stir in ½ tablespoon butter or smen and the finely sliced rind of ½ preserved lemon (see page 68). Serve with some spicy couscous.

QuickCook

Grills, Roasts, and Pan-Fries

Recipes listed by cooking time

3

2

10

3⏺ Moroccan Onion and Lamb Kebabs

Serves 4

2 large onions
1 teaspoon salt
2 teaspoons ras el hanout
2 tablespoons olive oil
juice of 1 lemon
1 lb shoulder of lamb,
    cut into bite-size chunks
bunch of flat leaf parsley,
    trimmed
lemon wedges, to serve

- Grate the onions into a large bowl, sprinkle with the salt, and let stand for 5 minutes. Tightly squeeze the onion into a nonmetallic bowl to extract the juice, then discard the grated onion.

- Stir the ras el hanout into the onion juice with the oil and lemon juice. Toss in the lamb and coat well, then let marinate for 15 minutes.

- Thread the marinated lamb onto 4 metal skewers and cook over a preheated barbecue grill or under a preheated broiler for 3–4 minutes on each side, until cooked through. Arrange the cooked kebabs on a flat serving dish, garnish with the parsley, and serve with lemon wedges to squeeze over the top.

 Broiled Lamb Cutlets with Bell Peppers and Onions Lightly brush 4 lamb cutlets, about 5 oz each, with a little olive oil and season. Cook under a preheated medium-hot broiler for 3–4 minutes on each side, until cooked through. Meanwhile, heat 2 tablespoons olive or argan oil in a heavy skillet, stir in 1 finely sliced onion, 1 cored, seeded, and finely sliced red or green bell pepper ,and 1 teaspoon sugar, and cook for 3–4 minutes. Toss in the finely chopped rind of ½ preserved lemon (see page 68), season well, and serve with the cooked lamb.

 Lamb, Bell Pepper, and Onion Kebabs Put 1 lb lean lamb, cut into bite-size chunks, in a nonmetallic bowl and toss with 2 tablespoons olive oil, the juice of 1 lemon, 2 crushed garlic cloves, and 1 teaspoon crushed cumin seeds. Let marinate for 10 minutes. Core, seed, and cut 2 red or green bell peppers into bite-size pieces and chop 1 onion into bite-size pieces. Thread the lamb onto 4 metal skewers, alternating with the bell peppers and onion, then cook over a preheated barbecue grill or under a preheated broiler for 3–4 minutes on each side, until cooked through. Season and serve with couscous and pickles.

10 Moroccan Onion and Cumin Beef Burgers

Serves 4

1 lb lean ground beef
1 onion, finely chopped
2 garlic cloves, crushed
2 teaspoons cumin seeds, crushed
1 teaspoon harissa paste
   (see page 70)
small bunch of flat leaf parsley,
   finely chopped
olive oil, for brushing
salt and black pepper

To serve

flatbreads
Moroccan pickles or chutneys

- Put the beef, onion, garlic, cumin seeds, harissa, and parsley into a bowl and season well. Knead the mixture well, lifting it up and slapping it back into the bowl until slightly sticky, then divide into 8 pieces and shape into firm patties.

- Lightly brush the patties with a little oil and cook over a preheated barbecue grill or under a preheated hot broiler for 3–4 minutes on each side, until cooked through. Serve with flatbreads and Moroccan pickles or chutneys.

---

2 **Chargrilled Onion and Cumin Beef Kebabs** Put 1 lb ground beef, 1 chopped onion, 2 crushed garlic cloves, 2 teaspoons ground cumin, 1 teaspoon cayenne powder, and a chopped small bunch of parsley in a bowl and season well. Knead the mixture as above, then divide into 4 and mold around 4 metal skewers. Brush with a little olive oil and cook over a preheated barbecue grill or under a preheated broiler for 4–5 minutes on each side, until cooked through. Toast 4 flatbreads for 1–2 minutes, then slit open. Slide the kebabs into the hollows and divide a bunch of cilantro leaves among them. Serve with harissa paste (see page 70) and yogurt.

3 **Onion and Cumin Beef Kebabs with Chickpea Puree** Put 1 (15 oz) can chickpeas, rinsed and drained, 2–3 tablespoons olive oil, the juice of 1 lemon, 1 garlic clove, and 1 teaspoon ground cumin into a food processor and process to a thick paste. Add 2 tablespoons plain yogurt, season, and process again, then transfer the mixture to an ovenproof dish. Drizzle with 1 tablespoon melted butter or ghee and put into a preheated oven, at 350°F, for 15 minutes, until lightly browned. Meanwhile, mix together 1 lb lean finely ground beef, 1 grated onion, and 2 teaspoons toasted and ground cumin seeds in a bowl.

Add 1 teaspoon caraway seeds, 1 teaspoon smoked paprika, ½ teaspoon cayenne or chili powder, and a finely chopped small bunch each of flat leaf parsley and cilantro and season well. Knead the mixture as above for 1–2 minutes, until smooth and slightly sticky. Divide into 4 and mold around 4 metal skewers. Lightly brush with olive or sunflower oil, then cook over a preheated barbecue grill or under a preheated broiler for 4–5 minutes on each side, or until cooked through. Garnish with extra herbs and serve immediately with the hot chickpea puree.

30 Fennel-Roasted Lamb with Honeyed Figs

Serves 4

3 garlic cloves, chopped
¼ cup peeled and chopped fresh ginger root
1 red chile, seeded and chopped
1 teaspoon sea salt
1 teaspoon ground coriander
1 teaspoon ground cumin
2 tablespoons smen, ghee, or softened butter
2 teaspoons fennel seeds
1½ lb lean loin of lamb
4 fresh figs, halved or quartered
2 tablespoons honey
salt and black pepper
small bunch of cilantro, finely chopped, to garnish
couscous, to serve (optional)

- Using a mortar and pestle, pound the garlic, ginger, chile, and salt to form a coarse paste, then add the ground spices. Beat the paste into the smen, ghee, or butter with the fennel seeds.

- Cut small incisions in the lamb and rub the mixture all over the meat, pressing it into the incisions. Put the lamb into a roasting pan and roast in a preheated oven, at 400°F, for 15 minutes.

- Baste the lamb with the cooking juices, arrange the figs around it, and drizzle with honey. Season, then return to the oven and cook for another 10 minutes, until cooked through. Garnish with the chopped cilantro and serve thickly sliced, with couscous, if desired.

 Roasted Fennel and Honey Figs

Cut 8 fresh figs into quarters, keeping the bottoms intact, and place in an ovenproof dish. Dab a little smen or butter into each one, sprinkle over 1 teaspoon fennel seeds, and drizzle with 1–2 tablespoons honey. Put into a preheated oven, at 400°F, for 8 minutes, until softened and the honey has melted. Serve with grilled and roasted meats.

 Honey and Fennel-Roasted Lamb Cutlets Put 1 tablespoon smen, ghee, or softened butter into a bowl and beat in 2 crushed garlic cloves and 2 teaspoons crushed fennel seeds, then season. Cut 1 lb loin of lamb into 4 cutlets and put into a roasting pan. Rub the fennel mixture over the meat and put into a preheated oven, at 400°F, for 15 minutes, until cooked through, turning them over halfway through and drizzling with 1 tablespoon honey. Serve with the juices spooned over the lamb and lemon wedges to squeeze over the top.

30 Spicy Chargrilled Meatballs with Toasted Coconut

Serves 4

1 teaspoon cumin seeds
1 teaspoon coriander seeds
¼ cup dried or freshly grated
   coconut
12 oz lean ground beef
1 small onion, finely chopped
2 garlic cloves, finely chopped
1 red chile, seeded and chopped
1 teaspoon ground cinnamon
salt and black pepper
small bunch of cilantro,
   finely chopped, to garnish

To serve

pita breads
lime wedges

- Dry-fry the seeds in a small, heavy skillet over medium heat for 1–2 minutes, until they emit a nutty aroma. Using a mortar and pestle or a spice grinder, grind to a powder. Dry-fry the coconut for 1–2 minutes, until it begins to brown, then transfer to a plate to cool.

- Mix together the beef, onion, garlic, chile, cinnamon, ground spices, and 3 tablespoons of the coconut and season well. Knead the mixture well for 1–2 minutes. Cover and chill for 10 minutes.

- Knead the mixture and roll into small balls. Thread onto 4 large or 8 small metal skewers and cook over a preheated barbecue grill or under a preheated broiler for 3–4 minutes on each side, until cooked through. Sprinkle with the remaining coconut and the chopped cilantro and serve with pita breads, with lime wedges to squeeze over the top.

 Pan-Fried Spiced Coconut and Dried Fruit Dry-fry 1 teaspoon each of cumin, coriander, fennel, and cardamom seeds in a large, heavy skillet over medium heat for 1 minute. Add 2–3 tablespoons finely sliced dried or fresh coconut for 1–2 minutes, until it emits a nutty aroma. Stir in 1 heaping tablespoon ghee or butter until melted, then stir in 2 tablespoons each of finely sliced pitted dates and dried apricots for 2–3 minutes. Sprinkle with 1 teaspoon ground cinnamon and a little salt. Serve hot with couscous or lamb.

 Chargrilled Coconut and Chile Meatballs Mix together 8 oz lean ground lamb, 1 finely chopped onion, 2 crushed garlic cloves, 1 seeded and finely chopped red chile, 2 tablespoons dried coconut, and 2 teaspoons ground cinnamon in a bowl and season. Knead the mixture well and roll into small balls, then thread onto 4 large or 8 small metal skewers. Brush with some olive oil and cook over a preheated barbecue grill or under a preheated broiler for 3–4 minutes on each side, until cooked through. Serve with lemon wedges to squeeze over the top.

30 Spicy Pan-Fried Liver, Prunes, and Onions

Serves 4

12 oz liver, trimmed and
  thinly sliced
2 tablespoons all-purpose flour
¼ cup ghee, smen or argan oil
2 teaspoons cumin seeds
1 teaspoon coriander seeds
1 teaspoon fennel seeds
6 cloves
2 cinnamon sticks
2 garlic cloves, finely chopped
1 red chile, seeded and sliced
2 red onions, finely sliced
1½ cups pitted dried prunes,
  finely sliced
2 tablespoons chopped cilantro
4 flatbreads
butter or ghee, for spreading
salt and black pepper
¼ cup yogurt, to serve

- Toss the liver in the flour. Heat 2 tablespoons of the ghee, smen, or oil in a heavy skillet, add the liver, and cook for 3–4 minutes, until browned all over and just cooked through. Season, then drain on paper towels, and set aside.

- Dry-fry the seeds in a heavy skillet over medium heat for 1–2 minutes, until they emit a nutty aroma. Stir in the remaining ghee, smen, or oil, add the cloves, cinnamon, garlic, chile, and onions, and cook for 4–5 minutes, until the onions are softened and beginning to brown.

- Add the prunes and cook for 1 minute, then add the chopped cilantro and liver and heat through for 3–4 minutes, stirring to coat well, then season.

- Meanwhile, lightly toast the flatbreads, spread with a little butter or ghee, and put onto 4 serving plates. Spoon the liver and prunes on top of each and serve with dollops of yogurt.

10 Quick Pan-Fried Spicy Liver

Heat 2 tablespoons olive or argan oil in a skillet, stir in 2 chopped garlic cloves, 1 seeded and chopped red chile, and 1–2 teaspoons cumin seeds and cook for 2 minutes. Toss in 12 oz trimmed, sliced, and floured liver and cook for 3–4 minutes. Season and stir in 1–2 tablespoons chopped cilantro. Spoon onto toasted flatbreads and serve with lemon wedges.

20 Liver Kebabs with Cilantro Onions

Heat 2 tablespoons ghee or argan oil in a heavy skillet, stir in 2 finely sliced onions and 1 teaspoon sugar, and cook for 3–4 minutes, until softened and golden brown. Toss in 2 tablespoons finely chopped cilantro and season. Cover and keep warm. Cut 8 oz trimmed liver into bite-size cubes and thread onto 4 large or 8 small metal skewers, alternating with 2 thinly sliced merguez or chorizo sausages. Lightly brush with a little olive oil and cook under a preheated hot broiler for 2–3 minutes on each side, until cooked through. Season and serve with the cilantro onions.

MOR-GRIL-CEA

30 Roasted Cinnamon Chicken Thighs and Plums

Serves 4

2 tablespoons olive or argan oil

1 tablespoon butter

8 chicken thighs

2 teaspoons coriander seeds

4 cinnamon sticks

2–3 dried red chiles

²/₃ cup white wine, chicken stock, or water

4–6 sweet plums, halved and pitted

1 tablespoon honey

1 teaspoon ground cinnamon

salt and black pepper

couscous or chunks of crusty bread, to serve (optional)

- Heat the oil and butter in a large, heavy skillet, add the chicken thighs, and brown for 2–3 minutes, turning once. Put into an ovenproof dish, pour the butter and oil over the thighs, and sprinkle the coriander seeds, cinnamon sticks, and chiles over and around them. Pour in the wine, stock, or water and season.

- Place in a preheated oven, at 350°F, for 15 minutes. Arrange the plums around the chicken, drizzle with the honey, and sprinkle with the ground cinnamon. Return to the oven and cook for another 10 minutes, until the chicken is cooked through. Serve with couscous or crusty bread, if desired.

 Broiled Cinnamon Chicken with Plum Sauce Cut 3 skinless chicken breasts, about 5 oz each, into 3–4 long pieces each and lightly brush with sunflower or olive oil. Cook under a preheated medium-hot broiler for 2–3 minutes, then turn the chicken over, brush lightly with more oil, and cook for another 2–3 minutes, until cooked through. Dust with 1–2 teaspoons ground cinnamon, season, and serve with prepared plum sauce for dipping.

Pan-Fried Cinnamon Chicken and Plums Heat 2 tablespoons ghee or argan oil in a large, heavy skillet, stir in 2–3 finely chopped garlic cloves, 1 finely chopped onion, ¼ cup peeled and finely chopped fresh ginger root, 1 teaspoon finely chopped dried red chile, 2 teaspoons fennel seeds, and 1 teaspoon sugar, and cook for 2–3 minutes, until the onion softens and begins to brown. Add 6 oz skinless, boneless chicken breasts, cut into bite-size chunks, and stir to coat well. Cover and cook over medium heat, stirring occasionally, for 8–10 minutes. Season and add 3 pitted and quartered plums and 1–2 teaspoons ground cinnamon. Cover and cook for another 5 minutes, until the chicken is cooked through. Garnish with a little finely chopped cilantro and serve with couscous.

3⃝ Roasted Honeyed Quince and Duck Legs

Serves 4

4 duck legs
3 tablespoons olive oil
2 tablespoons butter
¼ cup peeled and finely chopped
   fresh ginger root
1 large quince, cut into
   8 segments
juice of 1 lemon
2 tablespoons honey
2 teaspoons ground cinnamon
salt and black pepper
small bunch of cilantro,
   finely chopped, to garnish
couscous, to serve (optional)

- Rub the duck legs with 2 tablespoons of the oil, season, and put into a roasting pan. Put into a preheated oven, at 400°F, for 20 minutes.

- Meanwhile, heat the remaining oil and the butter in a heavy skillet, stir in the ginger, and cook for 1 minute. Add the quince segments and cook for 2–3 minutes on each side, until they are golden brown. Turn off the heat and pour the lemon juice over the quince.

- Pour off any excess fat from the duck legs and arrange the pieces of quince around them. Drizzle the honey over the duck and quince and sprinkle with the cinnamon. Return to the oven and cook for another 10 minutes, until the duck legs are cooked through. Garnish with the cilantro and serve with couscous, if desired.

1⃝ Chargrilled Honey and Sesame Duck Skewers Thread 6 oz skinless duck breasts, cut into thin strips, onto 4 large or 8 small metal skewers. Sprinkle with a little salt and cook over a preheated barbecue grill or under a preheated broiler for 2–3 minutes on each side, until just cooked through. Place on a plate and drizzle with 2 tablespoons warmed honey, then roll in a bowl of toasted sesame seeds. Serve at once.

2⃝ Pan-Fried Duck, Almond, and Honey Rice Pour 2½ cups water or chicken stock into a large saucepan and bring to a boil. Stir in 1 cup rinsed and drained long grain rice with 1 teaspoon salt. Bring back to a boil, then cook over medium heat for about 10 minutes, until the water has been absorbed, or according to the package directions. Turn off the heat, cover the pan with a clean dish towel, put on the lid, and let steam for 5 minutes. Meanwhile, heat 2 tablespoons ghee or olive oil in a large, heavy skillet, stir in 1 finely chopped onion, 2 finely chopped garlic cloves, and 2 teaspoons fennel seeds, and cook for 1–2 minutes. Add 2 tablespoons finely sliced blanched almonds and 6 oz diced skinless duck breasts and cook for 3–4 minutes, until just cooked through. Add 2 teaspoons ras el hanout and season. When ready, add the rice to the pan and mix well. Drizzle with 1–2 tablespoons honey, dust with 1 teaspoon ground cinnamon, and serve with yogurt and pickles.

MOR-GRIL-FYT

Pan-Fried Quails with Ginger and Grapes

Serves 4

2 tablespoons sunflower oil
4 tablespoons butter
4–6 oven-ready quails
½ cup peeled and finely chopped
    fresh ginger root
3 garlic cloves, finely chopped
1½ cups halved seedless green
    or red grapes
salt and black pepper
couscous, to serve

- Heat the oil and most of the butter in large, heavy skillet. Add the quails and brown on both sides for 4–5 minutes, then transfer to a plate.

- Stir the ginger and garlic into the pan, cook for 1–2 minutes, then toss in the grapes and season well. Return the quails to the pan, cover, and cook over medium heat for 20 minutes, or until cooked through. Serve with couscous.

Pan-Fried Quail Eggs with Ginger

Heat 1–2 tablespoons ghee or butter in a heavy skillet, stir in 12 shelled, hard-boiled quail eggs, and cook for 2–3 minutes. Season and dust with 1 teaspoon ground ginger. Serve hot with a dab of harissa paste (see page 70).

Roasted Quails with Ginger and

Grapes Whisk together the juice of 1 lemon and 2 tablespoons olive oil in a small bowl, then rub over 4–6 plucked and cleaned quails. Season and place in a roasting pan or ovenproof dish. Peel and cut ¾ inch piece fresh ginger root into matchsticks, sprinkle around the quail, and drizzle with a little more olive oil. Put into a preheated oven, at 375°F, for 10 minutes. Add 2–3 tablespoons halved seedless grapes and mix well with the ginger root. Return to the oven and cook for another 5–6 minutes, or until the quails are cooked through and lightly browned.

30 Chargrilled Harissa Chicken Wings with Burned Oranges

Serves 4

1 tablespoon harissa paste
(see page 70)
2 tablespoons olive oil
small bunch of cilantro,
finely chopped
8–12 chicken wings
salt
small bunch of flat leaf parsley,
coarsely chopped, to garnish

For the oranges

2 oranges, cut into quarters
2 tablespoons confectioners'
sugar

- In a bowl, beat the harissa into the oil, season with salt, and stir in the cilantro. Put the chicken wings into a dish and brush with the harissa oil. Cover and let marinate for 15 minutes.

- Cook the marinated wings over a preheated hot barbecue or under a preheated hot broiler, basting with any remaining harissa oil, for 3–4 minutes on each side, until cooked through.

- Meanwhile, dip the oranges into the confectioners' sugar and cook over the barbecue or under the broiler for about 2–3 minutes on each side, until slightly burned but not black.

- Serve the chicken and oranges garnished with the parsley.

---

10 Broiled Dukkah Chicken and Oranges with Harissa Dip

Brush 8 chicken wings with a little olive oil and toss in 2–3 tablespoons prepared dukkah spice mix. Cook under a preheated medium broiler with 1 orange, cut into wedges, for 3–4 minutes on each side, until cooked through. Meanwhile, mix together 2 tablespoons olive oil, the juice of ½ lemon, and 2 teaspoons harissa paste (see page 70) in a small bowl. Serve the dip with the chicken and oranges.

20 Broiled Harissa Chicken with

Dukkah Orange Dip In a small bowl, mix together 2 teaspoons harissa paste (see page 70), 2 teaspoons honey, and 1 tablespoon olive oil to form a smooth paste. Smear it over 8 chicken wings, then cover and let marinate for 10 minutes. Meanwhile, whisk together 2 tablespoons olive oil and the juice of 1 orange, then stir in 2 tablespoons dukkah spice mix (for homemade, see page 118). Cook the chicken under a preheated medium broiler for 3–4 minutes on each side, until cooked through. Serve immediately with the dukkah dip.

Chicken Livers and Pomegranate Syrup on Fried Bread

Serves 4

2–3 tablespoons olive or argan oil
1 tablespoon butter
4 slices of crusty bread
2–3 garlic cloves, finely chopped
1 dried red chile, finely chopped
1 teaspoon cumin seeds
1 teaspoon coriander seeds
1 lb chicken livers, trimmed
  and cut into chunks
2 tablespoons pomegranate syrup
salt and black pepper

To garnish

finely sliced or chopped rind of
  ½ preserved lemon (see page 68)
small bunch of flat leaf parsley,
  finely chopped

· Heat the oil and butter in a heavy skillet, add the bread slices, and sauté for 2–3 minutes on each side, until crisp and golden brown. Drain on paper towels and set aside.

· Stir the garlic, chile, and seeds into the skillet and cook for 2 minutes. Add the chicken livers and cook, stirring, for 3–4 minutes, until browned all over. Season and stir in the pomegranate syrup.

· Place the fried bread on a serving dish and spoon the chicken livers over the top. Garnish with the preserved lemon rind and parsley and serve.

Pan-Fried Chicken Livers and Pomegranate Syrup Trim and chop 12 oz chicken livers. Heat 2 tablespoons olive or argan oil and a little butter in a heavy skillet, stir in 2 crushed garlic cloves and 1 teaspoon coriander seeds, and cook for 1–2 minutes. Toss in the chicken livers and cook for 3–4 minutes, until browned all over, then stir in 1 tablespoon pomegranate syrup and season. Garnish with 2 teaspoons finely chopped preserved lemon rind (see page 68) and serve on toasted flatbreads.

Chicken Liver and Pomegranate Syrup Rice Heat 1 tablespoon ghee in a heavy saucepan, stir in 1 finely chopped onion, 4–6 cloves and 1 teaspoon sugar, and cook for 2–3 minutes, until the onion begins to brown. Stir in 1¼ cups rinsed and drained long grain rice, season, and pour in 2½ cups water. Bring to a boil and cook for 2–3 minutes, then reduce the heat and cook gently for 10–12 minutes, until the water has been absorbed, or according to the package directions. Turn off the heat, cover the pan with a clean dish towel, put on the lid, and let steam for 5–8 minutes. While the rice is steaming, heat 2 tablespoons ghee or smen in a separate heavy saucepan, stir in 1 finely chopped onion, 2 finely chopped garlic cloves, 1 teaspoon each of cumin seeds and coriander seeds, and cook for 2–3 minutes. Add 8 oz trimmed and diced chicken livers, coat well, and cook for 3–4 minutes, until they are browned all over, then stir in 1 tablespoon pomegranate syrup. Add the rice to the pan and mix well. Serve garnished with a finely chopped small bunch of cilantro.

MOR-GRIL-MYB

Broiled Red Snapper Fillets with Chermoula Sauce

Serves 4

4 whole red snapper, about
   4 oz each
oil, for greasing
small bunch of flat leaf parsley,
   coarsely chopped, to garnish
couscous, to serve

For the chermoula sauce

1 teaspoon saffron threads
2 teaspoons water
2–3 garlic cloves, chopped
1 red chile, seeded and chopped
1–2 teaspoons cumin seeds
1 teaspoon sea salt
¼ cup olive oil
juice of 1 lemon
small bunch of cilantro,
   finely chopped
black pepper

- To make the sauce, place the saffron in a small bowl with the measured water and let soak for 5 minutes. Using a mortar and pestle, pound the garlic, chile, cumin seeds, and salt to form a coarse paste. Gradually whisk in the oil and lemon juice, then stir in the cilantro and season with black pepper. Pour in the saffron water and mix well.

- Make 3–4 slashes on both sides of each fish, put onto an oiled broiler pan. and brush with a little of the sauce. Cook under a preheated hot broiler for 4–5 minutes, then turn, brush with a little more sauce, and cook for 3–4 minutes, or until cooked through.

- Meanwhile, heat the remaining sauce in a small saucepan. Place the fish in a serving dish, spoon the sauce over the top, and garnish with the parsley. Serve with couscous.

Chargrilled Red Snapper with Chermoula Rinse and pat dry 4 gutted red snappers, about 8–10 oz each, and brush with a litte melted ghee on one side of each fish. Cook over a preheated barbecue grill or under a preheated broiler for 3–4 minutes on each side, brushing with melted ghee when you turn the fish over. When cooked through, sprinkle with 1–2 teaspoons sumac and serve with prepared chermoula paste.

Grilled Red Snapper with Chermoula Dressing Rinse and pat dry 4 gutted red snappers, about 8–10 oz each, and season. Using a mortar and pestle, pound 2 chopped garlic cloves, 1 seeded and chopped green chile, 1 teaspoon coriander seeds, and a little sea salt to form a coarse paste. Whisk in 1 tablespoon olive oil, the juice of 1 lemon, and 1 tablespoon finely chopped cilantro. Set the dressing aside. Rinse and drain 2 handfuls of arugula leaves and arrange on a serving dish. Heat 1 tablespoon olive oil in a ridged grill pan or heavy skillet, tipping the pan to spread the oil over the bottom. Add the fish and cook for 4–5 minutes on each side or until cooked through. Place on the arugula leaves and drizzle with the chermoula dressing.

 # Roasted Chile and Preserved Lemon Sardines

Serves 4

3 garlic cloves, finely sliced

2 red chiles, seeded and finely sliced

finely sliced rind of 1 preserved lemon (see page 68)

3 tablespoons olive or argan oil

juice of 1 lemon

salt and black pepper

8 sardines, gutted and cleaned

small bunch of flat leaf parsley, finely chopped, to garnish

chunks of crusty bread, to serve (optional)

- Mix together the garlic, chiles, and preserved lemon rind in a bowl, then mix in the oil and lemon juice and season well.

- Spread some of the mixture over the bottom of an ovenproof dish. Put the sardines on top and spoon the remaining mixture over the fish. Put into a preheated oven, at 400°F, for 10–15 minutes or until the sardines are cooked.

- Transfer the sardines to a serving dish, spoon the juices over them, and garnish with the parsley. Serve with crusty bread, if desired.

10 **Chargrilled Tabil and Preserved Lemon Sardines** Rinse and pat dry 4–8 gutted sardines. Melt 2 tablespoons ghee in a small saucepan, then stir in 2 teaspoons tabil spice mix and the finely chopped rind of ½ preserved lemon (see page 68). Brush the sardines with the ghee and season well. Cook over a preheated barbecue grill or under a preheated broiler for 3–4 minutes on each side, until cooked through, brushing with the ghee when the fish is turned. Serve garnished with a finely chopped bunch of cilantro.

30 **Spiced and Preserved Lemon Chargrilled Sardines** Dry-fry 2 teaspoons each of cumin seeds and coriander seeds in a heavy skillet over medium heat for 1–2 minutes, until they emit a nutty aroma. Put them into a spice grinder and grind to a powder. Grate 1 onion into a bowl and add the powder with 1 teaspoon paprika, the finely chopped rind of 1 preserved lemon (see page 68), and a finely chopped small bunch of cilantro. Mix with 3 tablespoons olive oil and season well. Rinse and pat dry 4–8 gutted sardines and, using a small, sharp knife, make several slashes along each side. Smear over the onion mixture, pressing it into the cuts. Let marinate for 10 minutes. Cook over a preheated barbecue grill or under a preheated broiler for 3–4 minutes on each side, until cooked through, basting with any remaining marinade. Serve garnished with a finely chopped small bunch of cilantro and the finely sliced rind of ½ preserved lemon.

10 Seared Harissa Tuna Steaks

Serves 4

1 tablespoon olive oil, plus
  extra for oiling
1 teaspoon harissa paste
  (see page 70)
1 teaspoon honey
1 teaspoon sea salt
4 tuna steaks, about 5 oz each
small bunch of cilantro,
  finely chopped, to garnish

To serve

couscous
lemon wedges

- Mix together the oil, harissa, honey, and salt in a small bowl, then rub the mixture over the tuna.

- Heat a lightly oiled large ridged grill pan or heavy skillet until hot, add the tuna, and sear for 2 minutes on each side, until browned on the outside but still pink in the center. Garnish with the cilantro and serve with couscous, with lemon wedges to squeeze over the fish.

 2 Harissa Tuna Steaks with Pan-Fried Almonds Melt 2 tablespoons butter in a skillet, stir in 1–2 tablespoons slivered almonds, and cook for 2–3 minutes, until golden brown, then transfer to a bowl. Rub the grated rind of 1 orange into the almonds. Mix together 1 tablespoon olive oil and 2 teaspoons harissa paste (see page 70) in a small bowl, then lightly brush the mixture over 4 tuna steaks. Heat an oiled ridged grill pan or skillet, add the tuna, and cook for 3–4 minutes on each side, until browned on the outside but still pink in the middle. Season and serve with the almonds sprinkled on top.

 3 Pan-Fried Tuna and Harissa Onions Heat 2 tablespoons olive or argan oil in a heavy skillet, stir in 2 finely sliced onions, 2 finely chopped garlic cloves, 1 teaspoon coriander seeds, and 2–3 bay leaves, and cook for 1–2 minutes. Add the finely chopped rind of 1 fresh or preserved bitter orange, 1 teaspoon dried oregano, and 1 teaspoon sugar, cover, and cook over medium heat for 5–6 minutes, until the onions are softened. Remove the lid and continue to cook for 8–10 minutes, until the onions are soft and golden brown. Stir in 2 teaspoons harissa paste (see page 70), then add 4 tuna steaks, lifting the onion mixture over the top. Pour in about 1/3 cup white wine and cook for 6–8 minutes. Season well and serve garnished with a finely chopped small bunch of flat leaf parsley.

Swordfish, Bay, and Lime Kebabs

Serves 4

1 onion, grated

1–2 garlic cloves, crushed

2–3 teaspoons sumac

2 tablespoons olive oil

1 lb skinless swordfish, boned and cut into bite-size chunks

2 limes, cut into segments, plus extra to garnish

handful of fresh bay leaves

black pepper

- Mix together the onion, garlic, most of the sumac, and the oil in a shallow bowl. Season with black pepper, then toss in the swordfish and let marinate for 10 minutes.

- Thread the fish onto 4 metal skewers, alternating with the lime segments and bay leaves. Cook over a preheated barbecue grill or under a preheated broiler for 2–3 minutes on each side, until the swordfish is browned and cooked all the through. Sprinkle with the remaining sumac and serve immediately, with extra lime wedges to squeeze over the fish.

Swordfish, Bay, and Tomato Kebabs

with Lime Thread 10 oz skinless swordfish, boned and cut into bite-size pieces, onto 4 metal skewers, alternating with 12 cherry tomatoes and a handful of fresh bay leaves. Brush with melted ghee or butter, then cook over a preheated barbecue grill or under a preheated broiler for 3 minutes on each side, until the fish is cooked through, brushing with more melted ghee or butter. Sprinkle with 1–2 teaspoons sumac and serve with lime wedges.

Swordfish, Scallop, and Bay Kebabs

with Lime Place 12 scallops and 10 oz skinless swordfish, boned and cut into bite-size chunks, in a nonmetallic bowl. Using a mortar and pestle, pound 2 chopped garlic cloves, 1 seeded and chopped red chile, 1 teaspoon cumin seeds, 1 teaspoon coriander seeds, and 1 teaspoon sea salt to form a coarse paste. Whisk in 2 tablespoons olive oil and the juice of 2 limes. Pour the mixture over the swordfish and scallops and toss well. Cover and let marinate for 15 minutes. Thread the swordfish and scallops onto 4 metal skewers, adding a fresh bay leaf occasionally. Cook over a preheated barbecue grill or under a preheated broiler for 3–4 minutes on each side, until cooked through, basting with any remaining marinade. Serve immediately with lime wedges to squeeze over the top.

30 Grilled Turmeric Squid with Crushed Chickpeas

Serves 4

2–4 fresh squid
juice of 1 lemon
3 tablespoons melted ghee,
plus extra ghee for frying
1 onion, finely chopped
2 garlic cloves, finely chopped
1 red chile, seeded and
finely chopped
1 teaspoon cumin seeds
1 (15 oz) can chickpeas, rinsed
and drained
2–3 teaspoons turmeric
salt and black pepper
small bunch of flat leaf parsley,
finely chopped, to garnish
lemon wedges, to serve

- To prepare the squid, hold the body in one hand and tug the head firmly with the other, so that the head and innards are released all at once. Remove the transparent backbone and rinse the body sac inside and out. Sever the tentacles just above the eyes and trim if long. Cut the squid sacs in half lengthwise, score the inside with a knife in a diamond pattern, cut each half into 2 or 3 pieces, and put into a nonmetallic bowl with the lemon juice.

- Put 1 tablespoon of the ghee into a heavy skillet, stir in the onion, garlic, chile, and cumin seeds, and cook for 2–3 minutes. Stir in the chickpeas, mix well, and season, then crush gently with a potato masher. Drizzle with 1 tablespoon of the ghee, cover with aluminum foil, and keep warm.

- Pat the squid dry, then toss in the turmeric. Heat a ridged grill pan or heavy skillet until hot and add a little ghee, then cook the squid in batches for 2–3 minutes, until opaque and lightly browned. Season.

- Stir the remaining melted ghee into the crushed chickpeas and spoon onto a serving dish. Top with the squid, garnish with parsley, and serve with lemon wedges to squeeze over the top.

---

10 Simple Pan-Fried Turmeric Squid

Slice about 8–10 oz prepared fresh squid into thin strips. Pat dry and toss with 2 teaspoons turmeric. Heat 1–2 tablespoons olive oil or ghee in a large, heavy skillet, add the squid, and cook for 3–4 minutes, until opaque and lightly browned. Season and serve immediately with lime wedges to squeeze over the squid.

20 Pan-Fried Spicy Turmeric Baby Squid Prepare 8 baby squid by removing the head, innards, and transparent backbone. Rinse the squid sacs, pat dry, and sprinkle with 2 teaspoons turmeric. Heat 1 tablespoon olive oil or ghee in a large, heavy skillet, stir in 2 finely chopped garlic cloves and 1 tablespoon peeled and finely chopped fresh ginger root, and cook for 1–2 minutes, until just beginning to brown. Add the squid and cook for 2–3 minutes on each side, or until opaque. Add 1 tablespoon honey, the juice of 1 lemon, and 1–2 teaspoons harissa paste (see page 70) and cook gently for 4–5 minutes, until beginning to caramelize. Season with salt, sprinkle with a little finely chopped cilantro, and serve immediately.

20 Chargrilled Chile Shrimp with Lime

Serves 4

2 tablespoons chili oil
juice of 2 limes
2 tablespoons honey
½ teaspoon salt
12–16 raw shrimp, shells on
lime wedges, to serve

- Put the chili oil, lime juice, honey, and salt in a nonmetallic bowl and stir until the honey has dissolved. Slit the shrimp along their backs and pull out the black vein, then toss in the marinade, pushing it into the shells. Let marinate for 10 minutes.

- Thread the shrimp onto 4 metal skewers and cook over a preheated barbecue grill or under a preheated broiler for 2–3 minutes on each side, until they turn pink and are cooked through. Serve immediately with lime wedges to squeeze over the shrimp.

10 Pan-Fried Chile, Tabil, and Lime

Shrimp Heat 2 tablespoons ghee or argan oil in a heavy skillet, stir in 2–3 finely chopped garlic cloves and 1 seeded and finely chopped red chile, and cook for 2–3 minutes. Add 2 teaspoons tabil spice mix and 1 lb peeled shrimp, stir to coat well, and cook for 4–5 minutes, until they have turned pink and are cooked through. Stir in the juice of 1 lime and season. Serve with chunks of crusty bread and lime wedges to squeeze over the shrimp.

30 Roasted Chile and Lime Shrimp

and Carrots Put 8 peeled and grated carrots, 2 seeded and finely sliced green chiles, and 2 teaspoons cumin seeds in a roasting pan or ovenproof dish, then toss with 2–3 tablespoons olive oil. Put the carrots into a preheated oven, at 350°F, for 15–20 minutes. Place 12–16 large peeled shrimp on the carrots and add the juice of 2 limes. Return to the oven and cook for another 10 minutes, or until the shrimp turn pink and are cooked through. Toss all the ingredients together with 1 tablespoon finely chopped cilantro, season, and serve with chunks of crusty bread.

30 Mini Saffron Fish Balls

Serves 4

1 teaspoon saffron threads

1 lb skinless white fish fillets, boned and finely flaked

1 onion, finely chopped

1 red chile, seeded and finely chopped

finely chopped rind of 1 preserved lemon (see page 68)

bunch of cilantro, chopped

1 egg, beaten

sunflower oil, for frying

2 tablespoons dukkah spice mix (for homemade, see page 118)

salt and black pepper

lime wedges, to serve

- Using a mortar and pestle, grind the saffron to a powder and add a teaspoon of water. Place the fish in a bowl, add the saffron water, and rub in well. Add the onion, chile, preserved lemon rind, and cilantro and season. Mix well with a fork and stir in the egg. Knead the mixture until sticky, then roll into small balls.

- Heat enough oil in a large, heavy skillet for pan-frying, add the fish balls, and cook in batches over medium heat for 4–5 minutes, until golden brown and cooked through. Drain on paper towels, then toss with the dukkah in a bowl. Serve with lime wedges to squeeze over the fish balls.

---

1 Fish Burgers with Saffron Butter

Put 1 (5 oz) can tuna, drained, 4 chopped scallions, 2 teaspoons harissa paste (see page 70), 2–3 tablespoons fresh bread crumbs, and a chopped bunch of cilantro into a bowl. Add 1 beaten egg and mix well, then shape into 4 patties. Heat enough sunflower oil for frying in a skillet, add the burgers, and cook for 3–4 minutes on each side. Meanwhile, melt 1–2 tablespoons butter in a saucepan, then stir in a pinch of saffron. Place the burgers on toasted flatbreads, pour the saffron butter over them, and serve with chopped onions, herbs, and chutneys.

2 Fish Cakes with Saffron Lemon

Juice Mix together the juice of 2 lemons and a pinch of saffron threads in a small bowl and set aside. Dry-fry 1–2 tablespoons sunflower seeds in a heavy skillet over medium heat for 2 minutes, until they emit a nutty aroma. Put 1 (5 oz) can tuna, drained, into a bowl with 1 finely chopped onion, 2 teaspoons harissa paste (see page 70), a finely chopped small bunch of flat leaf parsley, and 1 beaten egg. Mix well with a fork, season, and add ¼ cup fine fresh bread crumbs. Knead the mixture, then roll into small balls. Flatten the balls in the palm of your hand, then lightly dip in all-purpose flour. Heat enough sunflower oil for pan-frying in a large, heavy skillet, add the fish cakes, and cook for 3–4 minutes on each side, until golden brown and heated through. Transfer to a serving dish and spoon the saffron lemon over the fish cakes. Serve immediately with couscous.

30 Chermoula Fish and Grape Leaf Skewers

Serves 4

3–4 skinless white fish fillets,
  about 6 oz each, such as halibut,
  or monkfish tails, boned
12–16 grape leaves in brine,
  drained and rinsed

For the chermoula

2–3 garlic cloves, chopped
1 red chile, seeded and chopped
1–2 teaspoons cumin seeds
1 teaspoon sea salt
small bunch of cilantro, chopped
¼ cup olive oil
juice of 1 lemon

To serve (optional)

lemon wedges
harissa paste (see page 70)

- Make the chermoula. Using a mortar and pestle, pound the garlic, chile, cumin seeds, and salt to a coarse paste. Add the cilantro and gradually whisk in the oil and lemon juice.

- Cut the fish fillets into 3–4 pieces each and put into a nonmetallic bowl. Stir in the chermoula and let marinate for 10 minutes.

- Place the grape leaves on a flat surface and put a piece of marinated fish in the center of each. Fold over the edges and wrap up into small packages. Thread onto 4 large or 8 small metal skewers and brush with any remaining marinade.

- Cook the skewers over a preheated barbecue grill or under a preheated broiler for 3–4 minutes on each side, until the fish is cooked through. Serve with lemon wedges to squeeze over the fish and a dab of harissa paste, if desired.

---

1 Cheese-Stuffed Grape Leaf Kebabs with Chermoula Dressing In a bowl, toss together 8 oz Muenster cheese, cut into 8–10 bite-size slices, 1–2 tablespoons olive oil, and 1–2 teaspoons smoked paprika. Place 8–10 grape leaves in brine, drained and rinsed, on a flat surface, put a cheese slice in the center of each, and fold over the edges to form tight packages. Thread onto 4 large or 8 small metal skewers and cook over a preheated barbecue grill or under a preheated broiler for 2–3 minutes on each side. Mix together 2 tablespoons olive oil, the juice of 1 lemon, and 1 tablespoon prepared chermoula paste in a bowl. Serve the kebabs drizzled with the chermoula dressing.

2 Chermoula Scallop and Grape Leaf Kebabs Put 12 scallops into a bowl, add 1 tablespoon olive or argan oil and 1 tablespoon prepared chermoula paste, and season. Toss and let marinate for 5 minutes. Place 12 vine leaves in brine, drained and rinsed, on a flat surface and put 1 marinated scallop in the center of each. Fold over the edges to form small packages, then thread onto 4 large or 8 small metal skewers. Cook over a preheated barbecue grill or under a preheated broiler for 3–4 minutes per side. Serve with lemon wedges to squeeze over.

30 Vegetable Kebabs with Harissa Yogurt

Serves 4

1 eggplant, cut into chunks
2 zucchini, cut into chunks
2 bell peppers, seeded and cubed
2 onions, cut into chunks
8–12 cherry tomatoes
2 tablespoons olive oil
juice of 1 lemon
2 garlic cloves, crushed
1 teaspoon ground coriander
1 teaspoon ground cinnamon
2 teaspoons honey
salt and black pepper

For the yogurt

1¾ cups plain yogurt
2 garlic cloves, crushed
2–3 teaspoons harissa paste
  (see page 70)
small bunch of cilantro, chopped
small bunch of mint, chopped

- Put all the vegetables and tomatoes into a nonmetallic bowl. Mix together the oil, lemon juice, garlic, ground spices, and honey in a small bowl, then season and pour the marinade over the vegetables. Toss well and let marinate for 5 minutes.

- To make the harissa yogurt, mix together the yogurt, garlic, and harissa in a separate bowl, season, and stir in the herbs, reserving some for garnish.

- Using your hands, toss the vegetables and tomatoes gently in the marinade, then thread alternately onto 8 metal skewers. Cook over a preheated barbecue grill or under a preheated broiler, brushing with any remaining marinade, for 3–4 minutes on each side, until browned and tender. Sprinkle with the reserved herbs and serve immediately with the harissa yogurt.

---

10 Tomato and Cheese Kebabs with Harissa Oil Thread 8 oz Muenster cheese, cut into chunks, and 12–16 cherry tomatoes onto metal skewers. Brush with 1 tablespoon melted ghee and cook over a preheated barbecue grill or under a preheated broiler for 2–3 minutes on each side, basting occasionally. Mix together 2–3 tablespoons olive or argan oil and 2 teaspoons harissa paste (see page 70) in a bowl. Season the kebabs, drizzle with the oil, and serve.

20 Roasted Vegetables with Harissa Yogurt Sprinkle 2 diced eggplants, 2 diced zucchini, 1 cored, seeded, and diced red bell pepper, and 1 diced onion in a roasting pan or ovenproof dish, add 3–4 smashed garlic cloves, 2 teaspoons coriander seeds, and a few thyme sprigs, and pour ¼ cup olive oil, the juice of 1 lemon, and 1–2 teaspoons sugar over the vegetables. Season and toss well. Put into a preheated oven, at 400°F, for 25 minutes, until the vegetables are tender and lightly browned. Meanwhile, make the Harissa Yogurt as above. Serve with the roasted vegetables.

20 Pan-Fried Citrus Carrots and Mango

Serves 4-6

1–2 tablespoons olive or argan oil

1 onion, finely chopped

¼ cup peeled and finely chopped fresh ginger root

2 garlic cloves, finely chopped

4–5 carrots, peeled and sliced

1 small, firm mango, peeled, pitted, and thickly diced

1–2 teaspoons ras el hanout

juice of 2 limes

2 tablespoons orange blossom water

small bunch of flat leaf parsley, finely chopped

salt and black pepper

lime wedges, to serve (optional)

- Heat the oil in a heavy skillet, stir in the onion, ginger, and garlic, and cook for 2–3 minutes. Add the carrots and cook for 3–4 minutes, until they begin to brown.

- Stir in the mango and ras el hanout. Add the lime juice and orange blossom water and cook gently for 4–5 minutes. Season, toss in half the parsley, and garnish with the rest. Serve hot, with lime wedges to squeeze over the carrots and mango, if desired.

---

10 Pan-Fried Spiced Dried Mango

Heat 1–2 tablespoons ghee in a heavy skillet, stir in 1 teaspoon cumin seeds, 2 teaspoons coriander seeds, and 2 crumbled bay leaves, and cook for 1–2 minutes. Toss in 2 cups dried mango, cut into thin strips, for 2–3 minutes and season with salt. Drain the mango on paper towels, then dust with 1 teaspoon ras el hanout. Serve hot.

30 Roasted Gingered Carrots and Mango

Sprinkle 4 peeled carrots, cut into matchsticks, and a thumb-size piece of fresh ginger root, peeled and cut into thin matchsticks, in an ovenproof dish. Tuck in 4–6 fresh or dried bay leaves and pour 2 tablespoons olive or argan oil over the carrots. Put into a preheated oven, at 400°F, for 15 minutes. Mix in 1 firm mango, peeled, pitted, and cut into matchsticks, season, and drizzle with 1 tablespoon honey. Return to the oven and cook for another 10 minutes. Serve with roasted meat and poultry.

MOR-GRIL-PEA

Baby Eggplants with Honey and Harissa

Serves 4

8 baby eggplants, halved
lengthwise or thickly sliced
3 tablespoons olive oil
2–3 garlic cloves, finely chopped
¼ cup peeled and finely chopped
fresh ginger root
2 teaspoons cumin seeds
1–2 teaspoons harissa paste
(see page 70)
¼ cup honey
juice of 1 lemon
1 cup water
salt and black pepper
small bunch of cilantro,
finely chopped, to garnish
flatbread, to serve

- Brush the eggplants with some of the oil and cook them under a preheated medium-hot broiler or in a ridged grill pan for 2–3 minutes on each side, until lightly browned.

- Heat the remaining oil in a heavy skillet, stir in the garlic, ginger, and cumin seeds, and cook for 2–3 minutes. Add the harissa, honey, and lemon juice and pour in the measured water. Stir well, then heat until simmering and add the eggplants. Reduce the heat and cook gently for about 10 minutes, until they have absorbed the sauce, adding more water, if necessary. Season.

- Garnish with a little cilantro and serve hot or at room temperature with flatbread.

---

10 **Deep-Fried Eggplants with Harissa Honey** In a deep saucepan, heat enough sunflower oil for deep-frying to 350–375°F or until a cube of bread browns in 30 seconds. Deep-fry the eggplant in the oil until golden brown. Melt 2 tablespoons honey in a small saucepan and stir in 1–2 teaspoons harissa paste (see page 70). Drain the eggplants on paper towels, then place on a serving dish and drizzle with the harissa honey. Garnish with a chopped small bunch of cilantro and serve with meats and poultry.

30 **Honey and Harissa Roasted Eggplants** Cut 2 eggplants in half and, using a sharp knife, carefully remove and chop the flesh. Brush the inside of the empty eggplant shells with a little olive oil, put into an ovenproof dish, and place in a preheated oven, at 350°F, for 4–5 minutes. Meanwhile, heat 2 tablespoons olive oil in a heavy skillet, stir in 1 finely chopped onion and 2 finely chopped garlic cloves, and cook for 1–2 minutes, then stir in the eggplant. Add 1 (14½ oz) can tomatoes, drained of juice, 1 tablespoon honey, 2 teaspoons harissa paste (see page 70), and a finely chopped small bunch of cilantro. Season well and stir in 2–3 tablespoons fresh bread crumbs, then spoon into the roasted eggplant shells and top with 2 thinly sliced tomatoes. Dab each with a little butter and bake in the oven for 20 minutes. Serve hot, garnished with a finely chopped small bunch of cilantro.

Roasted Cilantro and Preserved Lemon Potatoes

Serves 4

3 tablespoons ghee or butter

¼ cup finely chopped cilantro, plus extra to garnish

finely sliced rind of 1 preserved lemon (see page 68)

9 russet potatoes (about 2¼ lb), peeled and finely sliced

salt and black pepper

· Melt the ghee or butter in a small saucepan and stir in the cilantro and preserved lemon rind. Put the potatoes into a large bowl, pour the melted mixture over them, and toss the potatoes well to coat.

· Spread the coated potatoes in an ovenproof dish, season, and cover with aluminum foil. Place in a preheated oven, at 400°F, for 15 minutes. Remove the foil and return to the oven for another 10 minutes, until tender and lightly browned. Garnish with extra cilantro and serve with roasted or grilled meat, poultry, or fish.

Deep-Fried Cilantro and Preserved Lemon Potatoes

In a deep saucepan, heat enough sunflower or vegetable oil for deep-frying to 350–375°F or until a cube of bread browns in 30 seconds. Deep-fry 1½ lb new potatoes, peeled and finely sliced, in batches until golden brown. Mix together 1 tablespoon finely chopped cilantro and the finely chopped rind of 1 preserved lemon (see page 68). Drain the potatoes on paper towels, then place on a serving dish and sprinkle with the cilantro and preserved lemon.

Spicy Cilantro and Preserved Lemon

Potatoes Cook 1½ lb peeled new potatoes in a saucepan of boiling water for 7–10 minutes, or until just cooked. Drain and refresh under cold running water, then chop into bite-size pieces. Heat 2 tablespoons ghee in a large, heavy skillet, add 3–4 finely chopped garlic cloves, 1–2 seeded and finely chopped red or green chiles, 2 teaspoons cumin seeds, and 1 teaspoon coriander seeds, and cook for 2 minutes. Stir in 2 teaspoons turmeric, then add the potatoes and cook for 1–2 minutes, stirring to coat well. Add the juice of 1 lemon, 1 tablespoon finely chopped cilantro, and the finely chopped rind of 1 preserved lemon (see page 68). Cook gently for 3–4 minutes, until the potatoes have absorbed the flavors, then season. Garnish with a finely chopped small bunch of cilantro and serve with grilled and roasted meat, poultry, or fish.

30 Roasted Spiced Squash

Serves 4

2 teaspoons coriander seeds

2 teaspoons cumin seeds

2–3 garlic cloves

1–2 teaspoons sea salt

1 teaspoon finely chopped dried
red chile or cayenne powder

1 teaspoon ground cinnamon

1 teaspoon ground allspice

3 tablespoons olive or argan oil

1 squash, such as acorn,
butternut, or hubbard, or small
pumpkin, halved, seeded, and
cut into thin wedges

- Using a mortar and pestle, pound the coriander and cumin seeds, garlic, and salt to form a coarse paste. Stir in the chile or cayenne, cinnamon, and allspice, then mix in the oil.

- Rub the mixture over the squash wedges, then place, skin side down, in a roasting pan or ovenproof dish. Roast in a preheated oven, at 400°F, for 25 minutes, until tender. Serve with grilled or roasted meat dishes.

---

1 Roasted Pumpkin Seeds

Heat 1 tablespoon sunflower or argan oil in a small, heavy skillet, stir in about 1 cup dried pumpkin seeds, still in their shells with the fibers rubbed off. Toss over high heat for 3–4 minutes, then stir in 1 tablespoon ghee or butter and cook for another 3–4 minutes, until lightly browned. Toss in 1 teaspoon sea salt, then drain the seeds on paper towels. To eat, gently crack open the seed with your teeth, extract the kernel, and discard the shell.

2 Pan-Fried Spicy Squash

Heat 2 tablespoons ghee or argan oil in a heavy skillet, stir in 1 teaspoon each of fennel seeds and coriander seeds, and cook for 1–2 minutes. Add ½ cup peeled and finely chopped fresh ginger root and 1 seeded and finely chopped red chile and cook for another 1–2 minutes. Add 1 peeled, seeded, and diced acorn, butternut, or hubbard squash and toss well to coat, then pour in ½ cup water or enough to just cover the bottom of the skillet. Cover and cook gently for 10 minutes, until the squash is tender and the skillet is almost dry. Drizzle in 1–2 tablespoons honey, season, toss well, and cook gently for 4–5 minutes. Serve hot as a side dish, garnished with a finely chopped small bunch of cilantro.

 # Deep-Fried Plantain Chips with Zahtar

Serves 4

2 large, ripe plantains
sunflower oil, for deep-frying
coarse sea salt
1–2 tablespoons zahtar

- In a deep saucepan, heat enough oil for deep-frying to 350–375°F or until a cube of bread browns in 30 seconds.

- Meanwhile, to peel the plantains, use a sharp knife to chop off the ends, then slit the skins lengthwise and remove the peel in strips. Slice the plantains finely.

- Deep-fry the plantain in the oil in batches for 2–3 minutes, until golden brown. Remove with a slotted spoon and drain on paper towels, then sprinkle well with sea salt. Put the slices into a bowl, toss with the zahtar, and serve immediately.

 2 Deep-Fried Baby Plantains with Chermoula Using a mortar and pestle, pound 2 seeded and chopped red chiles, 2 chopped garlic cloves, and a little sea salt to form a coarse paste. Mix in 2–3 tablespoons olive oil, the juice of 1 lemon, 1–2 teaspoons honey, and 1 tablespoon finely chopped cilantro. Peel 2–3 baby plantains as above, then cut in half lengthwise. In a deep saucepan, heat enough sunflower oil for deep-frying to 350–375°F or until a cube of bread browns in 30 seconds. Deep-fry the plantains for 6–8 minutes, until just golden brown. Remove with a slotted spoon and drain on paper towels. Transfer to a plate and drizzle over the sauce.

 **3 Roasted Spicy Baby Plantains** Peel 4 baby plantains as above, then put into a saucepan, cover with water, and bring to a boil. Add 1 teaspoon salt and boil for 6–8 minutes. Drain and refresh under cold running water, then place in an ovenproof dish with 3–4 cinnamon sticks and 2–3 dried red chiles. Drizzle with 2 tablespoons melted butter, sprinkle with 1–2 teaspoons finely chopped dried red chile, and top with 1–2 tablespoons honey. Place in a preheated oven, at 350°F, for 15–20 minutes, until slightly caramelized. Serve with grilled or roasted poultry.

MOR-GRIL-ZAR

QuickCook

Sweet Snacks, Desserts, and Drinks

Recipes listed by cooking time

30

20

1 Watermelon, Rose Water, and Lemon Balm Salad

Serves 4

½ ripe watermelon or 1 large wedge (about 2 lb or 6 cups when prepared)

2–3 tablespoons rose water

1 tablespoon lemon balm or mint leaves, finely shredded, plus extra to decorate

confectioners' sugar, for dusting

- Remove the skin and seeds from the watermelon. Place the flesh on a plate to catch the juice and cut into bite-size cubes. Put the cubes into a shallow freezer-proof bowl and pour the juice over the fruit. Add the rose water and the shredded lemon balm or mint and toss gently.

- Chill in the freezer for at least 5 minutes. Just before serving, dust with confectioners' sugar and decorate with extra lemon balm or mint leaves.

2 Watermelon, Pomegranate, and Rose Water Salad

Put 1⅔ cups seeded and diced watermelon flesh into a freezer-proof bowl. Cut 2 ripe pomegranates into quarters then, holding them over the watermelon bowl to catch the juice, bend each quarter backward and flick the seeds into the bowl, leaving behind the white membrane and pith. Gently stir in 2–3 tablespoons rose water and 1–2 teaspoons granulated sugar, then chill in the freezer for 10 minutes before serving.

3 Watermelon and Rose Petal Conserve with Yogurt

Put 2¼ cups granulated sugar and ½ cup water in a heavy saucepan and slowly bring to a boil, stirring continuously until the sugar has dissolved. Add the rind, cut into thin strips, and juice of 1 lemon, 2 tablespoons rose water, and 1⅔ cups seeded and diced watermelon flesh. Bring to a boil, then reduce the heat and simmer gently for 15 minutes. Stir in 2 tablespoons fresh scented rose petals and cook gently for another 8–10 minutes. Serve with thick strained yogurt.

(The cooled conserve can also be stored in sealed sterilized jars in the refrigerator for a month.)

1 Orange Blossom and Cinnamon Orange Salad

Serves 4

5–6 ripe oranges

2 tablespoons orange
  blossom water

2 teaspoons confectioners' sugar

1 teaspoon ground cinnamon

- Using a sharp knife, remove the peel and pith from the oranges. Put the oranges onto a plate to catch the juice and thinly slice, removing any seeds. Arrange the orange slices in a serving dish.

- Put the orange juice into a bowl and stir in the orange blossom water. Pour the juice over the oranges, dust with confectioners' sugar, and sprinkle the cinnamon over the fruit. Serve immediately.

---

2 Oranges with Orange Blossom and Cinnamon Syrup Put the grated rind of 2 oranges, 1¼ cups water, 1 cup granulated sugar, and 2 cinnamon sticks in a small saucepan and bring to a boil, then boil for 2–3 minutes, stirring continuously until the sugar has dissolved. Stir in 2 tablespoons orange blossom water, reduce the heat, and cook gently for 10 minutes. Meanwhile, using a sharp knife, remove the peel and pith from the grated oranges and an extra 2–3 oranges, then thinly slice, removing the seeds. Cut the slices into quarters and put into a bowl. Pour the hot syrup over the fruit and let cool.

3 Baked Cinnamon Oranges Using a sharp knife, cut 2 ripe oranges in half horizontally, then separate the segments from the pith and remove the seeds. Place the 4 orange halves, cut side up, in an ovenproof dish. Mix together 1 tablespoon granulated sugar and 2 teaspoons ground cinnamon in a bowl, then sprinkle over the oranges. Dot each one with a pat of butter and place in a preheated oven, at 350°F, for 20–25 minutes. Dust with confectioners' sugar and serve hot with cream, yogurt, or ice cream.

30 Spiced Quince Jam

Serves 4

5 fresh quinces
squeeze of lemon juice
1¾ cups granulated sugar
1 cup water
2 cinnamon sticks
1 vanilla bean
2–3 star anise
6 cloves
2 strips of lemon rind
mini pancakes, to serve

- Peel and core each quince, then place in a bowl of water with the lemon juice to prevent discoloration.

- Place the sugar and measured water in a heavy saucepan and bring to a boil, stirring continuously until the sugar has dissolved. Add the spices and lemon rind, then reduce the heat and simmer gently for 2–3 minutes.

- Meanwhile, coarsely grate the quinces, then add to the syrup and simmer gently for another 15–20 minutes. Serve the hot jam spooned over mini pancakes. (The cooled jam can also be stored in sealed sterilized jars in the refrigerator for 1 month.)

---

10 Quinces with Clove Sugar Quarter and core 2 quinces, then finely slice each quarter. Put into a bowl and squeeze the juice of 1 lemon of the fruit. Sift 2–3 tablespoons confectioners' sugar and ½ teaspoon ground cloves into a small serving dish and serve with the quinces. To eat, dip the slices of quince into the sugar.

20 Poached Quinces in Clove Syrup PUt 1¼ cups water and ¾ cup granulated sugar in a heavy saucepan and bring to a boil, stirring continuously until the sugar has dissolved. Stir in the juice of ½ lemon, 2 tablespoons rose water, and 4–5 cloves and cook gently for 5 minutes to form a light syrup. Meanwhile, peel, core, and seed 2 large quinces, then cut into 6–8 thick segments and put into a bowl of water with a squeeze of lemon juice. Drain the quince segments, add them to the syrup, and poach gently for 15 minutes. Let cool slightly in the pan, then serve with thick cream, yogurt, or ice cream.

 # Date and Pistachio Truffles

Serves 4

1¾ cups shelled pistachio nuts
1½ cups chopped pitted dates
1 tablespoon orange blossom water
1 teaspoon ground cinnamon
1 tablespoon honey
¾ cup dry flaked coconut

- Dry-fry the pistachios in a heavy skillet over medium heat for 1–2 minutes, until they begin to brown and emit a nutty aroma. Put into a food processor with the dates and blend to a thick paste.

- Transfer the paste to a bowl and knead in the orange blossom water, cinnamon, and honey. Roll about 16 small pieces of the mixture into bite-size balls.

- Sprinkle the coconut onto a plate. Roll the truffles in the coconut until evenly coated. Serve with coffee or tea.

Stuffed Almond Dates

Mix together 1½ cups ground almonds (almond meal), ¼ cup sugar, and 1 tablespoon rose water in a bowl, then work to a smooth, soft paste, adding more rose water, if needed. Put 8 pitted whole dates on a plate and stuff each one with the almond paste. Press the stuffed dates gently to compress the filling, leaving them slightly open to reveal the paste. Serve with coffee or tea.

Mini Pistachio and Date Pastries

Put 9 pitted dates, 1 cup shelled pistachio nuts, and 1 teaspoon orange rind into a food processor and blend to a thick paste. Sift 1¾ cups all-purpose flour into a bowl, then, using your fingertips, rub in 1 stick butter, cut into small pieces. Add 1–2 tablespoons orange blossom water and work to a smooth, soft dough. Roll about 20 small pieces of the dough into balls. Hollow out each ball with your finger and pinch the sides to form a tiny pot. Fill each about three-quarters full with the date paste and pull over the dough to enclose the filling. Slightly flatten the balls, make a small dent on the tops with the back of a fork, and place on a lightly oiled baking sheet. Bake in a preheated oven, at 400°F, for 10–12 minutes, until lightly browned. Let cool until firm, then dust with confectioners' sugar and serve with coffee or tea.

3 Sweet Cinnamon, Pistachio, and Raisin Couscous

Serves 4

1½ cups fine couscous

2 teaspoons ground cinnamon, plus extra for dusting

½ teaspoon ground cloves

1–2 tablespoons sugar

1¼ cups boiling water

1 tablespoon sunflower oil

4 tablespoons butter

1 cup shelled unsalted pistachio nuts

2–3 tablespoons golden raisins or raisins

½ cup milk

½ cup heavy cream

¼ cup honey

- Put the couscous into a heatproof bowl and stir in the cinnamon, cloves, and sugar. Pour the boiling measured water over the grains, cover, and let stand for 10–15 minutes. Drizzle the oil over the couscous and, using your fingertips, rub it into separate the grains.

- Melt the butter in a heavy skillet, stir in the pistachios, and cook until they emit a nutty aroma. Add the golden raisins or raisins and cook until plump, then pour the mixture over the couscous. Toss well and spoon the couscous into 4 serving bowls.

- Meanwhile, heat the milk and cream in a small saucepan. Pour the liquid over the couscous and drizzle with the honey. Serve immediately, with a dusting of cinnamon.

 Sweet Cinnamon Couscous Balls

Put 2⅓ cups couscous into a heatproof bowl and just cover with boiling water. Cover with plastic wrap and let stand for 5 minutes, then fluff up with a fork. Let cool slightly, then with your fingers, rub the grains to loosen. Mold small pieces into balls, squeezing them together. Roll the balls in 2 tablespoons confectioners' sugar and dust with 1 teaspoon ground cinnamon.

 Sweet Cinnamon Couscous Pudding

Put 2 cups couscous into a heatproof bowl and stir in 1½ cups warm water. Cover and let stand for 10 minutes. Fluff up the couscous with a fork, then rub the grains between your fingers to separate them. Bring 1¼ cups milk to just below boiling point, then stir in 2–3 tablespoons packed light brown sugar until it has dissolved. Stir in the couscous and cook gently for 4–5 minutes. Dust the top with ground cinnamon and serve immediately for breakfast or as a snack.

30 Orange and Honey Puffs in Citrus Syrup

Serves 4

3 eggs
juice of 1 orange
grated rind of 2 oranges,
  plus extra to garnish
¼ cup sunflower oil, plus extra
  for deep-frying
2 tablespoons honey
2¾ cups all-purpose flour,
  plus extra for dusting
1 teaspoon baking powder

For the syrup

1 cup granulated sugar
1 cup water
juice of 1 lemon
1–2 tablespoons orange
  blossom water

- In a bowl, whisk together the eggs, orange juice, orange rind, and oil until frothy, then stir in the honey. Sift in 2⅓ cups of the flour and the baking powder and beat to form a thick batter.

- To make the syrup, put the sugar and measured water into a heavy saucepan and bring to a boil, stirring until the sugar has dissolved. Stir in the lemon juice, reduce the heat, and simmer for 10 minutes, until syrupy. Stir in the orange blossom water and simmer over low heat.

- Beat the remaining flour into the batter until it forms a pliable dough. Transfer to a lightly floured surface and roll out to about ¼ inch thick, pulling out the dough until it stops springing back. Using a 2–3 inch cutter, cut out about 16 circles.

- In a saucepan, heat enough oil for deep-frying to 350–375°F or until a cube of bread browns in 30 seconds. Deep-fry the dough in batches for 2–3 minutes, until puffed up and golden brown. Remove with a slotted spoon and drain on paper towels. Using tongs, dip the puffs into the syrup and serve immediately, garnished with grated orange rind.

 1 Ice Cream with Orange and Honey Sauce Put ½ cup water into a small saucepan and stir in 1 teaspoon cornstarch until it has dissolved. Add the grated rind and juice of 1 orange, 2–3 tablespoons orange blossom water, and 2 tablespoons honey, then bring to a boil over medium heat. Reduce the heat and simmer for 3–4 minutes. Serve spooned over vanilla ice cream.

 2 Orange and Honey Puffs in Cinnamon Sugar Make the Orange and Honey Puffs as above. In a large bowl, mix together 3 tablespoons granulated sugar and 2 teaspoons ground cinnamon. Transfer the drained puffs into the bowl, cover with a plate or lid, and shake well to coat. Serve the puffs with coffee or tea.

 Pistachio, Lime, and Coconut Cakes

Serves 4

1¾ cups shelled unsalted pistachio nuts

¾ cup dry coconut

1 cup firmly packed light brown sugar

grated rind and juice of 1 lime

2 eggs

2 egg yolks

confectioners' sugar, for dusting

- Place 12 paper cup cake liners on a baking sheet. Put the pistachios and coconut in a food processor and process until ground. Add the brown sugar, lime rind, and lime juice and blend to a paste. Add the eggs and egg yolks and blend until smooth.

- Drop 1 heaping tablespoon of the batter into each cupcake liner. Bake in a preheated oven, at 400°F, for 12–15 minutes, until slightly firm to the touch.

- Let the cakes cool slightly, then dust with confectioners' sugar and serve with coffee or tea.

 Pistachio, Lime, and Coconut Topped Ice Cream Dry-fry 2 cups shelled unsalted pistachio nuts in a heavy skillet over medium heat for 1–2 minutes, until they emit a nutty aroma. Toss in 2–3 tablespoons dry coconut and the grated rind of 1 lime and toast for 1 minute, then stir in 1 tablespoon ghee or butter until it melts. Add 1 tablespoon sugar and stir continuously until it has dissolved. Serve hot over vanilla ice cream.

 Coconut and Lime Cookies In a bowl, cream together 1 stick softened butter and ½ cup granulated sugar for 3–4 minutes, until light and fluffy. Beat in ¾ cup dry coconut, the grated rind of 1 lime, and 1 teaspoon lime juice, then beat in 1 egg. Sift in 1⅓ cups all-purpose flour, 1 teaspoon cream of tartar, ½ teaspoon baking soda, and a pinch of salt and, using your fingers, work to form a dough. Knead until smooth, then place on a piece of wax paper and roll into a cylinder about 2 inches in diameter. Tuck the paper around the dough and place in the freezer for 10–15 minutes. Cut the dough into thin slices and place on a lightly oiled baking sheet. Bake in a preheated oven, at 400°F, for 6–7 minutes. Transfer to a wire rack and let cool.

MOR-SWEE-ZAL

3⏲ Baked Honey, Cardamom, and Cinnamon Figs

Serves 4

12 ripe fresh figs
1 tablespoon ghee or butter,
 plus extra for greasing
2 teaspoons cardamom seeds
2 cinnamon sticks
grated rind of 1 lemon
4–5 tablespoons honey
yogurt, crème fraîche,
 or thick cream, to serve
confectioners' sugar, for dusting

- Cut each fig lengthwise into quarters, keeping the bottom intact, and place in a lightly greased ovenproof dish.

- Melt the ghee or butter in a small saucepan, stir in the cardamom seeds, cinnamon sticks, lemon rind, and honey and cook for 2 minutes, until bubbling. Pour the mixture evenly over the figs.

- Bake in a preheated oven, at 400°F, for 20 minutes. Serve dusted with confectioners' sugar accompanied by yogurt, crème fraîche, or thick cream dolloped into the middle of each fig.

 Creamy Figs with Cinnamon Honey
Place 8 ripe fresh figs on a plate and, using a small, sharp knife, cut a deep cross into the top of each one, keeping the bottom intact. Put a spoonful of thick cream or yogurt into the hollow and drizzle each one with 1 tablespoon honey. Dust with ground cinnamon and serve.

 Pancakes with Dried Fig, Cinnamon, and Anise Seed Jam Put 1¼ cups water and 1 cup granulated sugar into a heavy saucepan and bring to a boil, stirring continuously until the sugar has dissolved. Reduce the heat and simmer for 5 minutes, until the syrup begins to thicken. Stir in the juice of 1 lemon, 1 teaspoon ground cinnamon, 1 teaspoon ground anise seed, and 2 cups coarsely chopped dried figs. Bring to a boil, then reduce the heat and simmer for 12 minutes, until the figs are tender. Meanwhile, heat 4 prepared pancakes according to the package directions. Serve with the hot preserves and thick cream or yogurt. (The cooled jam can also be stored in sealed sterilized jars in the refrigerator for 1 month.)

30 Spicy Nut and Raisin Truffles

Serves 4

3 cups blanched almonds

2 cups walnuts

3 cups raisins

1 stick butter

1 cup honey

1 teaspoon ras el hanout

1 teaspoon ground cinnamon

½ teaspoon ground ginger

¼ cup sesame seeds

- Using a mortar and pestle or a food processor, pound or blend the nuts and raisins to a coarse paste.

- Melt the butter in a heavy saucepan, stir in the honey and spices, then add the paste. Stir over low heat until the mixture reaches a jamlike consistency. Turn off the heat and let cool.

- Using wet fingertips, roll about 25 small pieces of the mixture into truffle-size balls. Place the sesame seeds on a plate. Roll the truffles in the seeds until evenly coated and serve.

---

1 **Spicy Almond and Raisin Honey Yogurt** Melt 1½ cups honey in a small saucepan. Stir in 2 tablespoons raisins, 2 tablespoons halved blanched almonds, and ½ teaspoon ras el hanout. Bring to a boil, then remove from the heat, stir, and let cool slightly to let the flavors mingle. Spoon 2–3 tablespoons thick plain yogurt into each of 4 bowls and spoon the honey over the top.

2 **Baked Spicy Almond and Raisin Balls** Put 2 cups ground almonds (almond meal), ¾ cup granulated sugar, and the grated rind of 1 lemon in a food processor and blend with 2 tablespoons water. Add 1 teaspoon ground cinnamon and ½ teaspoon ras el hanout and blend again until the mixture forms a soft paste. Roll about 20 small pieces of the mixture into balls. Make a hollow in each with your finger, fill each with a

plump raisin, and close up to seal. Place the balls on a baking sheet lined with parchment paper and bake in a preheated oven, at 400°F, for 6–8 minutes, until lightly golden brown. Lightly dust with confectioners' sugar and let cool slightly before serving.

 Hot Spiced Dried Fruit Compote

Serves 4

1 cup granulated or firmly packed
   light brown sugar

4 cups water

2 cinnamon sticks

4–6 cloves

2 star anise

juice of 1 lime

¾ cup pitted dried prunes

¾ cup dried apricots

½ cup dried figs

⅔ cup blanched almonds

1 tablespoon sesame seeds

confectioners' sugar, for dusting

plain yogurt or cream,
   to serve

- Put the sugar and measured water into a heavy saucepan and bring to a boil, stirring continuously until the sugar has dissolved. Stir in the spices, reduce the heat, and simmer for 10 minutes. Stir in the lime juice, dried fruit, and almonds and cook gently for another 8 minutes.

- Meanwhile, in a small, heavy skillet, dry-fry the sesame seeds over medium heat for 1–2 minutes, until they emit a nutty aroma.

- Sprinkle the compote with the toasted seeds and dust with confectioners' sugar. Serve with yogurt or cream.

 Quick Dried Fruit Compote

Put 2 cups dried apricots, 2 cups pitted dried prunes, 1 cup golden raisins, and 1 cup blanched almonds into a bowl. Pour over enough water to just cover the fruit, then add 1 cup granulated sugar and 2–3 tablespoons orange blossom water and stir gently until the sugar has dissolved. Serve for breakfast or as a snack with couscous or pancakes.

 Spiced Dried Fruit and Wine Compote

Put 1 cups halved dried figs, 1½ cup dried apricots, and 1½ cups pitted dried prunes into an ovenproof dish. Add 2–3 cinnamon sticks, 4–6 cloves, and 2 dried bay leaves. Pour in 1¼ cups white wine and sprinkle with 1 tablespoon packed light brown sugar. Bake in a preheated oven, at 350°F, for 15 minutes. Toss the fruit well and sprinkle with 1 tablespoon packed light brown sugar, then return to the oven for another 10 minutes. Serve hot with yogurt, thick cream, or ice cream.

 Simple Fresh Fruit Kebabs

Serves 4

4 fresh apricots, halved
   and pitted
4 fresh figs, quartered
½ honeydew melon, peeled,
   seeded and cubed
thick wedge of watermelon,
   peeled, seeded and cubed
small bunch of mint leaves
2 limes, quartered
confectioners' sugar, for dusting

- Thread the fruit onto 8 metal skewers, sticks, or twigs, alternating with the mint leaves and finishing with the lime quarters.

- Dust the fruit with confectioners' sugar and serve, squeezing the lime over the fruit before eating.

 Chilled Rose Water Fruit Salad Peel, seed, and chop ½ honeydew melon and put into a freezer-proof bowl. Add 2 halved, pitted, and chopped peaches, 2 peeled, cored, and chopped pears, 2 sliced bananas, and the juice of 1 lemon and mix well. Add 1½ cups halved and pitted cherries, 1½ cups green grapes, and ¼ cup fresh pomegranate seeds. Stir in ¼ cup rose water, then chill in the freezer for 10 minutes. Dust with confectioners' sugar and serve.

 Poached Red Wine and Rose Water Fruit Peel, quarter, and core 2 apples and 3 pears. Slice each quarter in half and put into a bowl with a squeeze of lemon juice to prevent discoloration. Bring 2 cups red wine, ½ cup granulated sugar, 2 cinnamon sticks, and the rind of 1 lemon, cut into strips, to a boil in a heavy saucepan, stirring continuously until the sugar has dissolved. Add the apples and pears and bring to a boil, then reduce the heat and cook gently

for 12–15 minutes, until just tender. Add 8 halved, pitted, and quartered apricots and ¼ cup rose water and cook gently for another 8–10 minutes, until tender but still retaining a little bite. Dust with confectioners' sugar and serve hot with thick cream, yogurt, or ice cream.

MOR-SWEE-TAA

30 Baked Almond and Orange Blossom Apricots

Serves 4

12 fresh apricots
1⅓ cups blanched almonds
½ cup granulated sugar
3 tablespoons orange
  blossom water
1–2 tablespoons honey

- Using a sharp knife, slit open the apricots down one side and remove the pits.

- Put the almonds, sugar, and orange blossom water into a food processor and blend to a soft paste. Roll 12 small pieces of the paste into balls, then stuff into the apricots. Press the apricots gently to compress the filling and place in an ovenproof dish.

- Bake in a preheated oven, at 350°F, for 15 minutes. Drizzle the honey over the fruit, then return to the oven and cook for another 5–6 minutes. Serve hot or cold.

 Nut and Orange Blossom Dried Apricots Drain 3 cups dried apricots, soaked overnight in 4 cups water, and reserve the soaking liquid. Put one-third of the apricots into a food processor and blend to a puree with the soaking water. Add 2 tablespoons granulated sugar and 3 tablespoons orange blossom water, then pour the liquid over the remaining apricots in a bowl. Stir in 2 tablespoons coarsely chopped blanched almonds and 2 tablespoons coarsely chopped shelled pistachio nuts. Serve with ice cream or yogurt.

 Poached Orange Blossom and Almond Apricots Drain 2 cups dried apricots, soaked in 2½ cups water overnight, and put the soaking liquid into a saucepan with 1 cup granulated sugar. Bring to a boil, stirring continuously until the sugar has dissolved, then boil gently for another 4–5 minutes. Stir in 2–3 tablespoons orange blossom water, the drained apricots, and 2 tablespoons blanched almonds. Bring to a boil, then reduce the heat and cook gently for 12–15 minutes. Serve hot with pancakes and ice cream.

30 Semolina Pancakes with Honey

Serves 4

1¾ cup all-purpose flour, plus
extra for dusting
½ teaspoon salt
1¼ cups fine semolina
1¼ cups warm water
3 tablespoons melted ghee
¼–⅓ cup honey

- Sift the flour and salt into a bowl and stir in the semolina. Gradually pour in the measured water and mix to form a soft dough. Knead well for about 5 minutes, until smooth and pliable. Divide into 8 pieces and roll into ping pong-size balls. Place on a lightly floured surface, cover with a clean, damp dish towel, and let rest for 10 minutes.

- Flatten and stretch each ball into a thin circle about 7 inches in diameter. Brush with melted ghee and fold one-third of it into the middle, the next third overlapping it, and the final third on top, so that you end up with a square package. Flatten each package and roll or stretch to about 6 inches square.

- Heat a heavy flat griddle pan or skillet and brush with a little of the melted ghee. Add the pancakes in batches and cook, brushing with melted ghee, for about 2 minutes on each side, until browned.

- Heat the honey in a small saucepan and drizzle it over the pancakes. Serve for breakfast or as a hot snack.

 ### Quick Pancakes with Honey

Heat 4 store-bought pancakes according to the package directions. Meanwhile, heat ¼ cup honey in a small saucepan. Place the pancakes on 4 serving plates, drizzle with the honey, and serve immediately with a sprinkling of roasted chopped nuts or toasted coconut.

 ### Toasted Coconut and Honey Pancake

Stacks Sift 1 cup all-purpose flour and a pinch of salt into a bowl, make a well in the center, and pour in 1 beaten egg. Gradually add 1¼ cups milk and beat to a smooth batter. Beat in 1 teaspoon sunflower oil and set aside. Dry-fry ¼ cup dry coconut in a saucepan over medium heat for 2–3 minutes, until lightly browned and it emits a nutty aroma. Heat a nonstick pancake pan or skillet, wipe it with a little sunflower oil, and add a ladleful of the batter, swirling it around to form a thin layer. Cook for 1–2 minutes on each side, until golden brown. Transfer to a plate and keep warm. Repeat with the remaining batter, adding a little more oil, if necessary. Heat ¼–⅓ cup honey in a small saucepan and layer up the pancakes, sprinkling with the toasted coconut and drizzling a little honey over each one. Divide the stack into 4. Top with the remaining honey and toasted coconut and serve immediately.

10 Crystallized Rose Petals

Serves 4

2 egg whites
2–3 tablespoons superfine sugar
2 sweet-scented, opened roses

- Line a baking sheet with wax paper. In a spotlessly clean bowl, whisk the egg whites with a handheld electric mixer until stiff.

- Put the sugar onto a plate. Carefully pull the rose petals off the flower heads. Brush a rose petal with a little egg white, then dip into the sugar. Shake off any excess and place on the wax paper to dry. Repeat with the remaining rose petals.

- For best results, let stand for 1–2 hours, until completely dry. Peel off the paper, then use to decorate puddings, cakes, and milk drinks.

2 Concentrated Rose Syrup

Put 2¼ cups granulated sugar and 1 cup water into a heavy saucepan and bring to a boil, stirring continuously until the sugar has dissolved. Add the juice of ½ lemon and simmer for 5 minutes. Stir in ½ cup rose water and simmer for 4–5 minutes. Let cool in the pan, then pass through a strainer into a sterilized bottle or jar. To serve, put a few ice cubes into a glass, add 2–3 tablespoons rose syrup, and fill up with cold water. (The concentrated syrup can be stored in the refrigerator for 3–4 weeks.)

3 Rose Water Milk Pudding

In a small bowl, mix together 2 heaping tablespoons rice flour and ⅓ cup milk to form a loose paste. Set aside. Put 3 cups milk and ⅔ cup granulated sugar into a heavy saucepan and bring to a boil, stirring continuously until the sugar has dissolved. Reduce the heat and stir 1–2 spoonfuls of the hot milk into the rice flour paste, then transfer the mixture to the pan, stirring continuously to prevent any lumps from forming. Return to boiling point, then stir in 2–3 tablespoons rose water, reduce the heat to low, and simmer gently for 20 minutes, stirring occasionally, until thickened. Serve hot with a dusting of confectioners' sugar.

3⟡ Almond and Cinnamon Phyllo Coil

Serves 4

4½ cups ground almonds
(almond meal)

1½ cups granulated sugar

2 tablespoons ground cinnamon,
plus extra for dusting

2 tablespoons orange
blossom water

12 sheets phyllo dough,
thawed if frozen

4 tablespoons butter, melted

1 egg yolk mixed with
1 tablespoon water, to glaze

confectioners' sugar, for dusting

- Line a baking sheet with parchment paper. Put the almonds, sugar, cinnamon, and orange blossom water into a food processor and blend to a thick paste. Put a clean, damp dish towel over the phyllo dough to prevent them from drying out.

- Brush the top phyllo sheet with a little melted butter. Roll lumps of the almond paste into fingers, then place end to end in a line inside one edge of the dough. Tucking in the ends to enclose the filling, roll up to form a long roll about a thumb's-width thick. Place in the center of the prepared baking sheet, crease the roll like an accordion, then shape it into a coil. Repeat with the remaining sheets of phyllo, wrapping them tightly around the first coil.

- Brush the egg wash over the coil. Place in a preheated oven, at 400°F, for 20 minutes, until lightly browned. Dust with confectioners' sugar and a swirl of cinnamon. Serve warm or at room temperature.

 Toasted Almond and Cinnamon Strips Mix together 1¾ cups ground almonds (almond meal), 3 tablespoons granulated sugar, and 1 tablespoon ground cinnamon in a bowl. Add 1 tablespoon softened butter or ghee and work to a paste. Lightly toast 2–3 slices of wheat or white bread, crusts removed and cut into strips, on one side under a preheated broiler. Turn them over, smear with the almond paste, and toast for 2 minutes. Serve as a hot snack.

 Almond Phyllo Sticks Mix together 1¾ cups ground almonds (almond meal), ⅓ cup granulated sugar, the grated rind of 1 lemon, and 1 tablespoon softened butter. Cut 8 sheets phyllo dough into rectangular strips and place under a clean, damp dish towel to prevent them from drying out. Brush a little melted butter over a phyllo strip, then put 1 heaping teaspoon of the almond mixture at one end, fold over the long sides, and roll up into a small cigar shape. Place on a lightly oiled baking sheet. Repeat with the remaining ingredients, making 16–20 sticks. Bake in a preheated oven, at 400°F, for 10–12 minutes. Dust with confectioners' sugar and serve warm.

3⦿ Almond and Toasted Sesame Seed Milk Pudding

Serves 4

1 cup blanched almonds
4 cups milk
¼ cup rice flour
¼ cup water
½ cup granulated sugar
1–2 tablespoons sesame seeds
a few drops of almond extract

- Put the almonds into a food processor and process until finely ground. Set aside. Heat the milk in a heavy saucepan to boiling point. Mix the rice flour with the measured water in a small bowl to form a smooth, thick paste. Take the milk off the heat and stir 2 tablespoons of the hot milk into the rice flour paste, then put the mixture back into the milk, stirring continuously to prevent any lumps from forming.

- Return to the heat and cook gently, stirring continuously, for about 5 minutes, until the mixture begins to thicken. Add the ground almonds and sugar and cook gently for another 15–20 minutes, stirring occasionally, until thick. Meanwhile, dry-fry the sesame seeds in a small, heavy skillet over medium heat for 1–2 minutes, until they emit a nutty aroma.

- Stir the almond extract into the milk pudding, then pour into 4 serving bowls and sprinkle with the toasted seeds. Serve hot or chilled.

1⦿ Almond and Sesame Seed

Snaps Dry-fry 1½ cups blanched almonds, chopped, over medium heat for 2–3 minutes. Put into a bowl. Add 1½ cups sesame seeds to the pan and dry-fry for 1–2 minutes. Add to the almonds. Put ½ cup honey and ⅔ cup granulated sugar into a saucepan, bring to a boil, and boil for 2 minutes, stirring continuously. Remove from the heat and stir in the almonds and seeds, then spread on an oiled baking sheet. Let cool, then loosen around the edges and break into pieces.

2⦿ Almond and Sesame Seed Balls

Put 1¾ cups all-purpose flour and 1 cup whole-wheat flour into a heavy skillet over medium heat and stir continuously for 3–4 minutes, until light brown and toasted. Transfer to a bowl and stir in 1 cup confectioners' sugar, sifted, and 2 teaspoons ground cinnamon. Dry-fry 1½ cups blanched almonds for 2–3 minutes, until golden brown, and remove, then dry-fry 1½ cups sesame seeds for 1–2 minutes, until they emit a nutty aroma. Put both into a food processor and process until finely ground, then add to the flour. Mix together 1 stick butter, melted, and 2 tablespoons honey, then combine with the flour and nuts. Roll small pieces of the mixture into cherry-size balls, then roll in confectioners' sugar. Press a slivered blanched almond into each one and serve with coffee or tea.

3 ⦾ Saffron Pears with Honey and Lavender

Serves 4

1¼ cups water

juice of 1 lemon

3–4 tablespoons honey

1 cinnamon stick

pinch of saffron threads

2–3 dried lavender heads, plus extra to decorate

4 firm pears, such as Bosc, with the stems intact, peeled

- Place the measured water and lemon juice in a heavy saucepan and bring to a boil. Stir in the honey, cinnamon stick, saffron threads, and lavender heads and cook gently for 5 minutes.

- Add the pears and bring to a boil, then reduce the heat and cook gently for 20 minutes, turning and basting frequently. Serve hot with the cooking liquid drizzled over the fruit, decorated with a few lavender petals.

 Saffron, Pear, and Lavender Tisane Place 4 tall, heatproof glasses on a tray and pour 1 tablespoon boiling water into each. Sprinkle 3–4 saffron threads into each glass and let steep for 2–3 minutes. Add 1 dried pear and 1 lavender stem to each glass. Fill up with boiling water, drizzle in 1–2 teaspoons honey to taste, and serve as a digestive drink at the end of a meal, or as a pick-me-up drink at any time of day.

 Ice Cream with Saffron Syrup and Lavender Put 2¼ cups granulated sugar, 1 cup water, and a pinch of saffron threads into a heavy saucepan. Let steep for 5 minutes, then bring to a boil, stirring continuously, until the sugar has dissolved. Reduce the heat and simmer for 10–12 minutes, until the syrup coats the back of a wooden spoon. Spoon the syrup over vanilla ice cream and serve sprinkled with a few lavender petals. (The cooled syrup can also be strained into a sterilized bottle or jar, sealed, and stored in the refrigerator for 3–4 weeks.)

30 Grapefruit and Pomegranate Salad with Mint Yogurt

Serves 4

2 ruby grapefruit
2 white grapefruit
2 ripe pomegranates, quartered
2 tablespoons orange
   blossom water

For the yogurt

1¼ cups thick plain yogurt
small bunch of mint leaves,
   finely chopped, plus a few
   leaves to decorate
2 tablespoons honey

- Put the yogurt into a bowl, fold in the mint, and swirl in the honey. Cover and chill in the refrigerator.

- Using a sharp knife, remove the peel and pith from the grapefruit. Holding the grapefruit over a bowl to catch the juice, cut down between the membranes and remove the segments, then put into a serving dish.

- Holding the pomegranate quarters over a plate to catch the juice, bend each quarter backward and flick the seeds into a bowl, leaving behind the white membrane and pith. Reserve 1 tablespoon of the seeds for decoration and sprinkle the rest over the grapefruit segments.

- Pour any grapefruit or pomegranate juice over the fruit with the orange blossom water and chill for 10–15 minutes in the freezer.

- Sprinkle the fruit with the reserved pomegranate seeds and mint leaves. Serve with the yogurt.

---

10 Pomegranate and Orange Juice

Remove the seeds from 2 pomegranates as above, put into a food processor with ⅔ cup water, and process to a puree. Add 2–3 drops of red food coloring. Pass through a strainer into a small bowl, then stir in the juice of 2 oranges and 2 tablespoons orange blossom water. Add sugar to taste, pour into 4 glasses, and decorate with a few mint leaves.

20 Pomegranate Syrup Tea

Cut 4–5 pomegranates in half horizontally and press on a lemon juicer to extract the juice. Put 1¼ cups of the juice and 1¾ cups granulated sugar in a heavy saucepan and bring to a boil, stirring continuously, until the sugar has dissolved. Reduce the heat and simmer for 10 minutes. Add 2 drops of red food coloring and simmer for another 2–3 minutes. To serve hot, spoon a little of the syrup into 4 heatproof cups and fill up with boiling water. To serve cold, pour a little of the syrup over some ice cubes in a glass and fill up with cold water. (The cooled syrup can also be strained into a sterilized bottle or jar, sealed, and stored in the refrigerator for 3–4 weeks.)

 # Dates with Rose Water and Milk

Serves 4

8 pitted dates
1/3 cup rose water
1/4 cup chilled milk
rose petals, to decorate

- Put the dates into a shallow bowl, pour 2–3 tablespoons of the rose water over the fruit, cover, and chill for 10–15 minutes.

- Drain the dates and pat dry with paper towels, then put into a serving dish. Put the remaining rose water and the milk into separate small glass or ceramic bowls.

- Arrange the dates, rose water, and milk on a tray and decorate with rose petals. To eat, first dip a date in the rose water, then into the milk. Serve with tea.

 **Date Syrup and Rose Water Tahini Paste** Put about 1½ cups tahini (sesame seed paste) in a bowl and beat until smooth. Add ¼ cup date syrup and mix well, then drizzle with 1 tablespoon rose water. Serve for breakfast with chunks of crusty bread for dipping, or spoon over toasted flatbreads or pancakes.

 Stuffed Date and Rose Water Fudge Put 16 pitted dates on a work surface and place a walnut half into each opening, then pack closely in a lightly greased, shallow baking dish. Melt 2 sticks butter in a saucepan, add 2 tablespoons granulated sugar and 2 tablespoons honey, and stir continuously for 2–3 minutes, until the sugar has dissolved. Beat in 2 cups all-purpose flour and stir over low heat for 5–6 minutes, until the mixture begins to turn light brown. Beat in 2 tablespoons rose water, then pour the mixture over the dates, filling in any gaps, and let set for 15–20 minutes. Cut into small squares, dust with confectioners' sugar, and serve with coffee or tea.

30 Strained Yogurt with Honeycomb

Serves 4

4 cups thick plain yogurt, such as
  Greek yogurt
8 oz fresh honeycomb
ground cinnamon, for dusting

- Line a strainer with a large piece of cheesecloth so that the edges flop over the sides, then place over a bowl. Add the yogurt to the cloth and let drip for 25 minutes. Transfer the strained yogurt to a bowl and beat until smooth and creamy.

- Spoon the yogurt into 4 serving bowls. Divide the honeycomb between the bowls and drizzle any loose honey over the top. Dust with cinnamon and serve immediately.

1 Ginger and Honey Yogurt

Put 1¾ cup thick plain yogurt into a bowl. Squeeze ¼ cup peeled and chopped fresh ginger root, through a garlic press, in batches to extract the juice, holding the press over the yogurt. Beat the juice into the yogurt and swirl in 2 tablespoons honey. Serve for breakfast or as a snack.

2 Spiced Honey Yogurt

Put ⅓ cup honey, the juice of 1 lemon, 2 cinnamon sticks, 1 teaspoon cardamom seeds, 2 star anise, and 5–6 peppercorns in a heavy saucepan and bring to a boil, then reduce the heat and simmer gently for 5 minutes. Let cool in the pan to let the flavors mingle. Spoon 2–3 tablespoons thick plain yogurt into each of 4 serving bowls. Pass the honey mixture through a strainer and pour over the yogurt. Serve for breakfast or as a snack.

MOR-SWEE-XAG

30 Chilled Almond Milk

Serves 4

2 cups blanched almonds
2½ cups water
½ cup granulated sugar
1 tablespoon orange
   blossom water
ice cubes, to serve

- Put the almonds into a food processor and blend to a smooth paste, adding a splash of water to loosen.

- Put the measured water and sugar into a heavy saucepan and bring to a boil, stirring continuously until the sugar has dissolved. Stir in the almond paste and simmer for 5 minutes. Stir in the orange blossom water and turn off the heat.

- Let cool in the pan to let the flavors mingle, then pass through a cheesecloth into a small bowl and squeeze tightly to extract all the milky liquid from the almonds.

- Pour into 4 glasses, add some ice cubes to each, and serve immediately. Alternatively, chill the glasses in the refrigerator or freezer.

---

1 Chilled Yogurt Drink Beat 1¾ cups chilled, thick plain yogurt in a bowl until smooth. Gradually pour in 2 cups chilled water, beating continuously, then add salt to taste. Put a few ice cubes into 4 glasses and pour in the yogurt. Sprinkle a little dried mint over each one and serve with spicy food.

2 Chilled Vanilla Milk Put 2½ cups milk and 2 vanilla beans into a heavy saucepan and bring to just below boiling point. Turn off the heat, stir in sugar to taste, and let cool. Remove the vanilla beans, slit open lengthwise, and scrape out the seeds. Strain the milk into a small bowl, stir in the seeds, and pour into 4 glasses over ice cubes. Alternatively, chill in the refrigerator before serving.

MOR-SWEE-FYO

Moroccan Mint Tea with Lemon Verbena

Serves 4

2 teaspoons Chinese Gunpowder green tea leaves

2–3 sugar lumps, plus extra to taste

large bunch of peppermint and garden mint leaves and stems

small bunch of lemon verbena leaves and stems

- Place the green tea and sugar lumps in a teapot. Pour in a little boiling water and let steep for 5 minutes.

- Stuff the mint and lemon verbena leaves into the pot, packing them in as tightly as you can. Add more sugar lumps to taste—the sugar enhances the flavor of the mint—and fill up the pot with boiling water.

- Put the teapot over a pan of boiling water, like a double boiler, or over low heat on the stove. Let the tea brew for 10 minutes.

- Place 4 tea glasses on a tray. Pour some of the tea into a glass, then tip it back into the pot. Hold the pot high above the glasses and pour slowly so that bubbles form on top of the tea. Serve immediately.

Quick Peppermint Tea

Trim several stems of peppermint to the size of your tea glasses. Place 1–2 leafy stems into each of 4 glasses with 1–2 sugar cubes or 1–2 teaspoons honey to taste. Fill each glass with boiling water, cover with a clean dish towel, and let steep for 2–3 minutes. Serve hot.

Iced Orange Mint Tea

Using a mortar and pestle, bruise a large bunch of peppermint, spearmint, and garden mint leaves with 2 tablespoons granulated sugar. Add the sliced rind of 1 orange and bruise with the mint to release the flavors. Transfer the orange and mint mixture to a heavy saucepan, add 2 tablespoons green tea leaves, 2–4 tablespoons granulated sugar, and 2½ cups water, and bring to a boil, stirring continuously until the sugar has dissolved. Reduce the heat and simmer for 2–3 minutes. Stir in the juice of 2 oranges and the juice of 1 lime. Let cool in the pan. Strain into a small bowl and chill in the freezer for 10–15 minutes. To serve, fill 4 tall glasses with crushed ice, pour in the chilled te,a and decorate with a slice of orange and a slice of lime.

Hot Spicy Tea with Chiles

Serves 4

2 cinnamon sticks

¼ cup peeled and finely sliced
 fresh ginger root

6 cloves

4 dried red chiles

2½ cups water

2–3 tablespoons honey

1 lemon, cut into 4 thick slices

- Put the spices and the measured water into a medium saucepan and bring to a boil. Reduce the heat and cook gently for 15 minutes. Stir in the honey and simmer for another 3–4 minutes.

- Strain the tea into 4 heatproof glasses, add 1 of the chiles to each, and serve with a slice of lemon.

 Quick Ginger and Chile Tea

Put 4 thick slices of peeled fresh ginger root, 4 dried red chiles, and 2 cups boiling water into a saucepan and boil gently for 8–10 minutes. Strain the tea into 4 heatproof glasses, add 1 of the chiles to each, and sweeten with honey to taste.

 Spiced Ras el Hanout Milky Tea

Put 1¼ cups milk, 2 cinnamon sticks, 4 thick slices of peeled fresh ginger root, and 2 star anise in a saucepan and bring to just below boiling point. Stir in 1–2 teaspoons ras el hanout. Turn off the heat and let steep for 10–15 minutes. Meanwhile, put 1 tablespoon black tea leaves into a heatproof bowl, pour in 1¼ cups boiling water, and let steep for 10 minutes. Pour the tea into the milk and bring to just below boiling point. Stir in 2–4 tablespoons honey to taste, then reduce the heat and simmer for 10 minutes. Strain the tea into a teapot and serve immediately in heated teacups.

 # Moroccan Coffee with Cardamom

Serves 4

4 coffee cups of water,
   about ½ cup each
4 cardamom pods
4 teaspoons finely ground
   Arabica coffee
4 teaspoons sugar

- Put the measured water and cardamom pods into a small saucepan and carefully spoon the coffee and sugar on top. Gently stir the sugar and coffee into the surface of the water, making sure you don't touch the bottom of the pan with the spoon.

- Bring to just below boiling point over medium heat, gradually drawing in the outer edges of the coffee into the middle to create a froth. Just as the coffee is about to bubble, spoon some of the froth into 4 coffee cups and pour in the coffee. Let stand for 1 minute before drinking to let the coffee grains settle at the bottom of the cups.

 ### Milky Cinnamon Coffee

Put 2 tablespoons finely ground coffee, 4 cinnamon sticks, and 1¾ cups water in a saucepan and bring to a boil, stirring continuously, then turn off the heat and let steep for 10 minutes. Strain the coffee, reserving the cinnamon sticks. Pour back into the pan and heat gently to just below boiling point. Put ¾ cup condensed milk into a separate pan and heat gently to just below boiling point. Place the reserved cinnamon sticks into 4 cups, mugs, or heatproof glasses. Pour in the coffee to just over halfway, then pour in the condensed milk. Dust the tops with ground cinnamon and serve immediately.

 ### Iced Cardamom and Cinnamon

Coffee Put 2 tablespoons finely ground coffee, 4 cinnamon sticks, 8 cardamom pods, and 1 cup water into a saucepan and bring to just below boiling point. Turn off the heat and let cool. Meanwhile, in a separate pan, heat 1 cup water and 1 cup granulated or firmly packed light brown sugar, stirring continuously, until the sugar has dissolved. Boil for 2–3 minutes, then reduce the heat and simmer for 5 minutes. Stir in the coffee and let cool. Strain into a small bowl, reserving the cinnamon sticks and cardamom pods, and chill in the freezer for 10–15 minutes. Put the reserved cardamom pods and cinnamon sticks into 4 tall glasses, fill them with crushed ice, and pour the chilled coffee over the ice. Serve immediately.

Index

Page references in *italics*
indicate photographs

Acknowledgments

Recipes by Ghillie Basan
Executive Editor Eleanor Maxfield
Senior Editor Leanne Bryan
Copy Editor Jo Murray
Americanizer Theresa Bebbington
Art Direction Tracy Killick and Geoff Fennell for Tracy Killick Art Direction and Design
Original design concept www.gradedesign.com
Designer Tracy Killick and Geoff Fennell for Tracy Killick Art Direction and Design
Photographer Will Heap
Home Economist Sunil Vijayakar
Prop Stylist Liz Hippisley
Production Allison Gonsalves